MEDICAL PRACTICE

Body of Knowledge Review

VOLUME 4

Governance and Organizational Dynamics

Stephen L. Wagner, PhD, FACMPE

Managing Editor

Lawrence F. Wolper, MBA, FACMPE

Medical Group
Management
Association

Medical Group Management Association
104 Inverness Terrace East
Englewood, CO 80112-5306
877.275.6462
Website: www.mgma.com

Medical Group Management Association (MGMA) publications are intended to provide current and accurate information and are designed to assist readers in becoming more familiar with the subject matter covered. Such publications are distributed with the understanding that MGMA does not render any legal, accounting, or other professional advice that may be construed as specifically applicable to an individual situation. No representations or warranties are made concerning the application of legal or other principles discussed by the authors to any specific factual situation, nor is any prediction made concerning how any particular judge, government official, or other person will interpret or apply such principles. Specific factual situations should be discussed with professional advisors.

Production Credits
Executive Editor: Andrea M. Rossiter, FACMPE
Managing Editor: Lawrence F. Wolper, MBA, FACMPE
Editorial Director: Marilee E. Aust
Production Editor: Marti A. Cox, MLIS
Page Design, Composition and Production: Boulder Bookworks
Substantive and Copy Editor: Sandra Rush, Rush Services
Proofreaders: Scott Vickers, InstEdit and Mara Gaiser
Fact Checking: Mary S. Mourar, MLS
Cover Design: Ian Serff, Serff Creative Group, Inc.

Portions of this volume were excerpted from "Organization and Operations of Medical Group Practice," pp. 39–44 by Stephen L. Wagner in *Physician Practice Management: Essential Operational and Financial Knowledge*, Lawrence F. Wolper, ed. (Sudbury, Mass.: Jones and Bartlett Publishers, Inc., © 2005). Reprinted with permission.

PUBLISHER'S CATALOGING IN PUBLICATION DATA

Wagner, Stephen L.
    Governance and organizational dynamics / by Stephen L. Wagner ; managing editor Lawrence F. Wolper. – Englewood, CO : MGMA, 2006.
    131 p. : 13 ill. ; cm. – (Medical Practice Management Body of Knowledge Review Series ; v. 4)
Includes bibliographical references and index.
ISBN 1-56829-240-6
    1. Group practice governance. 2. Decision Making, Organizational (MeSH). 3. Practice Management, Medical – organization & administration [MeSH]. 4. Organizational change [LC]. I. Wolper, Lawrence F. II. Medical Group Management Association. III. American College of Medical Practice Executives. IV. Series. V. Series: Body of Knowledge Review Series.

R728.W34 2006
610.6821.W34—dc22   2005938794

Item 6360

ISBN: 1-56829-240-6   Library of Congress Control Number: 2005938794

Printed in the United States of America
10 9 8 7 6 5 4 3 2 1

Acknowledgments

I would like to thank
Michele N. Wurschmidt and Elizabeth A. Wagner
for their help in the preparation
of this manuscript.

Contents

Series Overview

THE MEDICAL GROUP MANAGEMENT ASSOCIATION (MGMA) serves medical practices of all sizes, as well as management services organizations, integrated delivery systems, and ambulatory surgery centers to assist members with information, education, networking, and advocacy. Through the American College of Medical Practice Executives® (ACMPE®), MGMA's standard-setting and certification body, the organization provides board certification and Fellowship in medical practice management and supports those seeking to advance their careers.

■ **Core Learning Series: A professional development pathway for competency and excellence in medical practice management**

Medical practice management is one of the fastest-growing and most rewarding careers in health care administration. It is also one of the most demanding, requiring a breadth of skills and knowledge unique to the group practice environment. For these reasons, MGMA and ACMPE have created a comprehensive series of learning resources, customized to meet the specific professional development needs of medical practice managers: the *Medical Practice Management Core Learning Series*.

The Medical Practice Management Core Learning Series is a structured approach that enables practice administrators and staff to build the core knowledge and skills required for career success. Series resources include seminars, Web-based education programs, books, and online assessment tools. These resources provide a strong, expansive foundation for managing myriad job responsibilities and daily challenges.

■ Core Learning Series: Resources for understanding medical practice operations

To gain a firm footing in medical practice management, executives need a broad understanding of the knowledge and skills required to do the job. The Medical Practice Management Core Learning Series offers "Level 1" resources, which provide an introduction to the essentials of medical practice management. As part of the learning process, professionals can use these resources to assess their current level of knowledge across all competency areas, identify gaps in their education or experience, and select areas in which to focus further study. The *Medical Practice Management Body of Knowledge Review Series* is considered to be a Core Learning Series – Level 1 resource.

Level 1 resources meet the professional development needs of individuals who are new to or considering a career in the field of medical practice management, assuming practice management responsibilities, or considering ACMPE board certification in medical practice management.

Also offered are Core Learning Series – Level 2 resources, which provide exposure to more advanced concepts in specific competency areas and their application to day-to-day operation of the medical practice. These resources meet the needs of individuals who have more experience in the field, who seek specialized knowledge in a particular area of medical practice management, and/or who are completing preparations for the ACMPE board certification examinations.

■ Core Learning Series: Resources to become board certified

Board certification and Fellowship in ACMPE are well-earned badges of professional achievement. The designations Certified Medical Practice Executive (CMPE) and Fellow in ACMPE (FACMPE) indicate that the professional has attained significant levels of expertise across the full range of the medical practice administrator's responsibilities. The Medical Practice Management Core Learning Series is MGMA's recommended learning system for certification preparation. With attainment of the CMPE designation, practice executives will be well positioned to excel in their careers through ACMPE Fellowship.

Preface

GOVERNANCE AND ORGANIZATIONAL DYNAMICS have become more important to all organizations in recent years. The modern medical group is no exception, and in a sense is in greater need for focused attention to this topic as health care comes under ever-increasing scrutiny. Rising costs, medical error and other quality concerns, potential conflicts of interest, and spiraling technology costs all add up to the need for much more attention to governance and organizational dynamics.

In a more practical sense, however, governance and organizational dynamics can be summed up as a need to *change and to protect the new status quo in a cycle of continuous improvement.* We are faced with the need for increasing change in an industry that is slow to embrace organizational change, but quick to adopt medical technology. The health care industry has many traditions that prevent change; for example, it values the individual to the exclusion of meaningful organizational development.

Those who work for change have few allies because many people are comfortable with the old status quo, others fear change will cost them their current advantage, and still others find their place in change uncertain. Regardless of the case, change is difficult. It requires an absolute commitment and active leadership. In the organizational setting, change can best be accomplished through an effective *governance* structure.

Organizational dynamics is the script for an organization's human capital. It is becoming clear in today's society that technical competence is a requirement. Nevertheless, it is not technology but customer service and other human interactions that define how we are perceived. Ironically, as much as health care is a business about the most important and intimate aspects of the human condition, the industry has often failed to properly focus on these relationships. It is imperative to fully explore and more fully understand and address these relationship issues with all of an organization's stakeholders, both internal and external.

Effective governance and the management of organizational dynamics are essential to a successful medical group and must have a higher priority in the future. This major challenge for medical group practices deserves much more attention.

Learning Objectives

AFTER READING THIS VOLUME, the medical practice executive will be able to:

1. Communicate the medical practice's mission, vision, values, and decisions to influence the practice's strategic direction;

2. Use negotiation skills to reach consensus on critical issues while maintaining trust and relationships with key constituents;

3. Resolve conflicts in ways that create energy and motivation for appropriate change in the medical practice;

4. Use assessment and/or survey tools to gain important data on stakeholders, situations, and personalities;

5. Display self-confidence and leadership skills to balance professional integrity and quality care with appropriate results for the practice;

6. Facilitate decision making, conflict resolution, strategic planning, and dialogue to move the medical practice forward;

7. Present information in an organized way by using appropriate media, settings, verbal and listening skills, and body language to gain attention and achieve specific objectives for the practice;

8. Plan for the future by setting goals and assigning responsibility and accountability to maximize individual and practice performance;

9. Build trust and relationships to motivate individuals and groups to become effective medical practice teams;

10. Use coaching methods to teach and reinforce desired performance;

11. Teach the benefits of standard business and financial practices to achieve quality patient care; and

12. Foster participation in self-assessment and continuous learning programs for everyone in the practice, including the administrator.

VIGNETTE **Seattle's ABC Practice**

A FEW YEARS AGO, Dr. John James, medical director of Seattle's ABC Practice, a multispecialty group practice, fought an uphill battle with the group's board to establish a managed care operation within the group. The managed care plan had been approved and implemented, but a substantial minority of the board remained bitterly opposed. The plan did well, but its profit margins were lower than the group's fee-for-service business. Just back from a national conference, Dr. James was convinced that the group must move as quickly as possible to forge an alliance with other providers in its service area to offer a wider range of services to potential patients and payers.

Dr. James feels that if the group does not move to control its future, it will almost certainly be an unwilling partner in some venture that others will put together. The problem, Dr. James knows, will be to gain the support of the board, so many of whose members are still smarting over the defeat – years later! How, he wonders, can he gain the necessary backing without repeating the earlier battle?

The major difficulty faced by Dr. James is, paradoxically, the result of his success in implementing the group's managed care plan. He clearly expended significant political capital in that war, as evidenced by the "substantial minority" of the board that opposed the plan in the final vote. It is likely that this group still has strong feelings about that defeat and is unlikely to allow another of Dr. James's proposals to proceed without its considerable input and consent.

Dr. James is clearly a knowledgeable and charismatic figure who has been able to move his initiatives forward on the strength of those characteristics, but his preparation of the group for change has been less than adequate. An attempt by Dr. James to implement another major initiative without additional consensus building is likely to lead to his ouster as medical director and CEO. He has realized that to be correct is not enough to get the organization to change and move forward.

Dr. James prepared himself to invest significant time and energy in creating a climate for change within the group and avoid attempting to push his new idea too vigorously. In addition, he was aware of the need to avoid being recognized as the author of this new undertaking and to instead allow the group to develop a sense of ownership of the concept of an alliance. Dr. James implemented this new initiative by undertaking the following strategy.

To reestablish his credibility as a decision maker, Dr. James reviewed the status of the group's managed care plan. He compared the group's position, both clinical and financial, before and after the plan's implementation and developed comparative statistics that confirmed the plan's success vis-à-vis other managed care products. Using his best political sense, he enlisted several of the board members who were opposed to the plan to assist in making a presentation to clinic physicians.

Once this was accomplished, he began to lay the groundwork for his new proposal. In addition, he felt this was a good time to review the group's mission statement, its goals, duties, and whether the structure of the group was adequate to achieve these goals. Using data from national organizations and other communities, Dr. James showed where the health care industry was going and where ABC Practice was currently positioned.

Knowing the support was essential, Dr. James identified board members who were opposed to the managed care plan and solicited their opinions early on about this new initiative. He arranged for several of them to attend meetings at which the development of an alliance was favorably discussed and had them each present a meeting summary to the group. He also met with as many board members as possible (one-on-one) and listened to their views.

Frequent communication pieces of increasing detail were provided to all members of the board, helping reinforce the support he received from other board members.

Dr. James was careful to ensure that appropriate structures were in place to support ABC Practice's major position in any alliance. This may require additional personnel, retraining existing personnel, and additional resources. Once he gained the commitment of the group, Dr. James developed a timetable for the transition and an educational program for all physicians and board members to ensure that all of his hard fought gains could be realized and maintained.

Dr. James taught the board that as trustees to ABC Practice, they must crystallize the role and function of their board so that they have the right board(s), with the right leaders, addressing the right issues in a timely manner, thereby enhancing the overall value of governance in the system. He was careful to point out that sometimes new board members operate, for a time, in a traditional fashion, while it could be more beneficial for them (and ABC) to assimilate more quickly into the current governance structure and function.

In evaluating the development of its governance structure and function, ABC Practice identified several factors that contribute to success:

- Board members understand their strong leadership and policy-making roles;
- Open avenues for communication among board members and key leaders;
- Good working relationships among board members, management, and support staff;
- The development of a shared vision. The leadership must often paint a compelling story of what is possible;
- Ongoing, regular communication among the CEO, board chair(s), and officers;
- Educating constituents about emerging health care issues;
- Extensive and consistent board and CEO evaluation processes; and

- A centrally coordinated function for governance that helps integrate the board(s) across the organization.

Dr. James reminded the group that a professionally driven governance function also elevates the importance of board within the organization.

Governance and Organizational Dynamics and the General Competencies

The *ACMPE Guide to the Body of Knowledge for Medical Practice Executives* defines five general areas of competency for the medical practice executive:

1. *Professionalism* – achieving and preserving professional standards;

2. *Leadership* – supporting the organization's strategic direction;

3. *Communication Skills* – interacting and presenting information clearly and concisely;

4. *Organizational and Analytical Skills* – solving problems, making decisions, and developing systems; and

5. *Technical Professional Knowledge and Skills* – developing the knowledge base and skill set necessary to perform activities unique to the job, role, or task.

Governance and organizational dynamics are areas that touch all of these competencies, as well as all of the other aspects of medical group administration, operations, and management. Without a mastery of governance and organizational dynamics, success in leading a medical group practice is unimaginable. Governance is the foundation of how the practice will behave, compete, and document its actions. The governance process leads to and controls the organizational dynamics of the group and thereby sets the stage for the group's positive interactions with patients, the community, referring providers, government, payers, vendors, hospitals, employees, and all other stakeholders. It can be as simple as a policy on e-mail use and as complicated as how the practice will interact with the community it serves.

Unlike some areas of necessary competency, it is not possible to outsource governance and organizational dynamics. The nature of group governance is tantamount to the nature of the group itself. Indeed, the need for a functional governance body is paramount to the success of the modern medical group practice.

Current Governance and Organizational Dynamics Issues

IT IS NOT SURPRISING that many medical groups have not developed the talent and skill base for optimal governance and organizational dynamics. Those competencies were largely irrelevant in the past, when groups were small and operated like family businesses. Most groups gave little thought to governance, simply meeting as a group when issues needed to be decided and making decisions as a group on an ad hoc basis. A group might even have chosen to ignore an issue altogether; there was no need for policies, procedures, or assessments. The group simply worked with one another every day, all day. Little was unknown or not discussed. It would have been a little like asking your spouse to meet and discuss family policy or requiring family discussions to follow Robert's Rules of Order.[1]

Governance and organizational dynamics have now become increasingly significant issues in group practice administration, and this significance continues to grow. The governance of medical group practices, rather passive in earlier times, now is becoming crucial to a practice's success. In the past, the environment was more stable and medical groups were more focused on technical competencies; today, technical competencies are not enough to sustain a medical group. The environment is changing, especially with ever-increasing demands being placed on the group practice and the health care system as a whole. More service, higher quality, and complex technology are all significant drivers of health care today. Medical practices today are dealing with a dynamic and diverse population, which adds to the complexity of the environment as well. Expectations are high, and medical groups, like all health care organizations, must respond with better performance. The strategic direction of performance in a complex organization, such as a medical practice, is the responsibility of governance through the management of the intricate interrelationships of all of its members and stakeholders.

There has also been great reluctance to change and to develop more formal organizational models and governance procedures. This, too, is no surprise. With size, though, comes diversity of thought, personality, and perspective, not to mention the need for new skills and knowledge in the areas of:

1. Correct selection of group members;

2. Policy and procedure;

3. Leadership and governance; and

4. Attention to organizational dynamics and a functional culture that places value on what advances the organization's mission.

Knowledge Needs

GOVERNANCE AND ORGANIZATIONAL DYNAMICS are about the management of stakeholder relationships. Many specific skills and knowledge elements must be mastered and effectively employed by the medical practice executive. Some examples include:

- Using operational dashboards to gain important information about the practice's current state and immediate future;

- Coaching all members of the board, staff, and physicians to teach and reinforce desired performance;

- Maintaining and building trust and relationships with key constituents by using negotiation skills;

- Resolving conflicts and facilitating decision making, conflict resolution, strategic planning, and dialogue to move the medical practice forward;

- Planning for the future, setting goals, and assigning responsibility and accountability to maximize performance;

- Communicating the medical practice's mission, vision, values, and decisions to influence its strategic direction; and

- Displaying self-confidence and leadership skills to balance professional integrity and quality care with appropriate results for the practice.

Overview of Governance and Organizational Dynamics Tasks

MEDICAL PRACTICE EXECUTIVES should develop and use their knowledge and skills to ensure that the following tasks related to governance and organizational dynamics are carried out.

■ TASK 1: **Lead and manage the organizational change process for practice improvement**

Change management has become synonymous with leadership in today's modern medical group practice. Change is inherently difficult and requires a clear understanding of culture, personalities, and a number of problem-solving skills. Coaching, mentoring, and helping individuals understand their own impacts on the organization are also necessary skills to manage expectation and properly establish performance measures for the group. Goals and measurements need to be established in a way that is consistent with the mission and vision of the medical group practice.

This all requires a clear knowledge of leadership and the operations of the group from a variety of viewpoints. By viewing problems and issues from many perspectives, it is possible to help each individual see his or her role in the medical group organization. Careful leadership, motivation, and trust building with all members and constituents are essential.

TASK 2: **Construct and maintain governance systems**

Strategic planning is relatively new but nevertheless is vital to medical group practice administration. This new and important task is the responsibility of the group's governing body. The board or other governing body must help the group evaluate itself and its environment by using a number of methodologies and tools. The purpose of this evaluation is to aid in achieving the desired outcomes for the group. Data must be collected and filtered against a series of requirements. In addition, these data must be turned into an understandable program or initiative for further evaluation and ultimate approval, to gain the group's support. Once plans are implemented, it is incumbent on the board to monitor and review the process against the organization's goals.

Organizing the activities of the medical group practice into coherent and effective committees, working groups, and accountable units is no small task. This requires effective administrative and physician teams who understand their roles and how they must come together into a single focused organization that speaks with one voice and expresses common goals and values. Building working relationships that function over time makes each member of the group a valued contributor who complements the work of the others.

Communicating well to such a wide variety of constituents is an essential skill for the medical practice executive. In addition to the formal methods of communication that must be used, the skilled executive knows the importance of the informal ways that communication works in the group. The skilled executive uses all pathways effectively to promote understanding and to reduce conflict.

■ TASK 3: **Evaluate and improve governing bylaws, policies, and processes**

Form vs. function is an old biological expression for the reality that the structure of an organ or body part is often well suited to its use. So, too, are the governance and organizational dynamic structures that are essential to the proper functions of the medical group. Without structure, it is impossible to effectively disseminate policies and procedures and to present the organization's mission in a purposeful way.

The medical practice executive must create and maintain an increasing number of documents that are necessary for the proper operation of the group. These documents are also to be used to prevent legal jeopardy for the group.

Selecting legal help can be critical. Getting well-intentioned and effective board members can be difficult. Good intentions are not enough; members of the board must be trained, and that training must be considered an ongoing and necessary element of the governance process. The well-known Peter Principle says that those who are excellent and competent at their jobs are often put into unfamiliar situations. Often the result is failure. Medical group practice governance is a textbook example of this phenomenon. Just because an individual is a great physician does not mean she or he has the skills or the ability, let alone the time, to govern a complex organization. It is essential that the medical practice executive assist in the development and understanding of the group. It is essential that members be trained. The group at large needs to understand the importance and the difficulty of this task. Who, what, and how are the watchwords for this task.

The group's history should not be ignored, because history provides richness. The group's stories about its development can serve as an inspiration and a point of cohesion for the group. The governing body of the medical group should also serve as the group's historian. It is simply easier to know where the practice is going if it knows where it has been.

■ TASK 4: Conduct stakeholder needs assessment and facilitate relationship development

Understanding need is often difficult. In the absence of objectively obtained information, we assume too much and relate to issues from our own perspectives. This task requires the executive to have an in-depth knowledge of surveying and the ability to interpret such data. As is often stated, the medical practice is a relationship business, and knowing its constituents is imperative. Community surveys and environmental scanning help the medical practice executive evaluate needs and opportunities. Such data also provide information for decision making at all levels of the organization.

Personal interaction is very important as well. Only 30 percent of meaning is conveyed by words. In today's world, it is important to remember that the personal touch often is still the best way to understand what is relevant and what is going on within the medical group practice.

Education of internal and external stakeholders is a continuing responsibility for the medical practice executive. It is important to develop the skills and content necessary for this task and to look for the opportunities, times, and places most conducive to presenting the medical group's story and message.

■ TASK 5: Facilitate staff development and teaming

The governing process of the medical group needs to promote the idea of a learning organization. Many models exist for effective group training. Computer-based methods, videos, interactive software, presentations, role playing, group discussion, books, and seminars are all ways to provide learning experiences. It is important as well to create a culture of learning in which the group values learning and provides the resources necessary to fulfill these educational needs. Incentives to learn are essential. In the modern environment, an organization that is incapable of learning is at a distinct disadvantage. Innovators are learners because learning is fundamental to adaptation, and innovators must adapt.

Staff development also involves endeavors that are less formal. Celebrating success and other accomplishments reinforces these values and helps engender a positive working environment. Employees should also be evaluated in part on their ability to innovate and manage change, both as individuals and as members of teams.

The group's mind-set needs to be understood and managed for an effective organization to succeed. The human dynamics of a medical group can be intense and counterproductive at times. Attention has to be paid to the emotional health of the group to prevent burnout and disruptive interaction with the staff. Executives and other leaders in the group need to seek opportunities to reduce stress and prevent unnecessary turnover. Developing leaders to help group members see the world in constructive ways prevents the victim mentality often seen today. So many of the current issues affecting a group are seemingly beyond the group's control, so leaders need to paint a compelling vision of the future for their followers. Regardless of the situation, the way an organization responds as a team should be managed by the leadership and the governing body of the medical group practice.

■ TASK 6: Facilitate physician understanding and acceptance of good business management

In years past, poor business practices would reduce the effectiveness of the organization; today, they can mean risking survival itself. The governing body of the group must be in tune with and understand proper business techniques and it must understand that these techniques are necessary for meeting group goals and fulfilling the needs of the group. This task requires leaders who must also be good teachers. Most clinical staff members are not trained in good business practices and therefore must be helped to understand the relevance and importance of these practices.

These optimal business practices go far beyond financial statements and tax returns. Understanding the patients' needs and working to exceed their expectations is important. Community involvement is also essential. The group cannot serve or optimally respond to a community it doesn't understand.

There are currently three or four generations in the workforce, with differing values, needs, and motivational characteristics. Workforce planning and training at the group leadership level can help the physicians understand their roles in employee satisfaction. Such activities can reduce turnover, and lower turnover is essential to the optimal operation of the group. The modern medical group must understand and respond to these challenges if it is to enjoy the full benefit of this diversity.

■ TASK 7: Develop and implement quality assurance programs

Health care quality has been an area of much scrutiny since the Institute of Medicine published its report, "To Err Is Human."[2] The quality of health care, however, depends on a lot more than clinical competency. It requires an effective organization that values clinical quality and has been structured to provide it. It all starts with the building of a team that is dedicated to the delivery of quality care.

It is also not enough in our modern health care environment to simply *think* we are good, it must be documented and measured. The Health Plan Employer Data and Information Set (HEDIS®), National Committee for Quality Assurance (NCQA), Joint Commission on Accreditation of Healthcare Organizations (JCAHO), and many other accrediting bodies assist with organizing and documenting the level of care provided by medical groups. Expertise in this area is becoming increasingly important as a management competency for group practice executives and other leaders in medical groups.

The proper understanding and execution of the financial aspects of the practice can hardly be understated. After all, "no money, no mission." Staff must be trained to understand the business and financial affairs of group practice in the various aspects of the practice. This is a task that requires extensive training and continuing education because billing, payment rules, and policies change regularly. By having proper records of revenues and expenses, budgets, and profit-and-loss statements, the governing bodies of the group can effectively monitor the fiscal well-being of the group; therefore, such data must always be accurate, consistent, and timely.

The use of forecasting tools will become increasingly important in the development and management of the turbulent fiscal environment surrounding health care. That turbulence will certainly continue for the foreseeable future, and medical groups must develop the ability to predict and react to these changes.

TASK 1 **Lead and Manage the Organizational Change Process for Practice Improvement**

■ Group Dynamics and Group Culture

Group culture will come up often in any discussion of group governance and organizational dynamics because culture (or the absence of culture) lies at the center of change and decision making. Simply stated, *organizational culture* is how things are done in an organization – its beliefs, patterns of behavior, shared values, and traditions.

The culture of an organization comes from a variety of sources. For the medical group, some of those sources are:

1. Professional training;

2. Traditions of the group;

3. The cult of personality;

4. The specialty and type of group;

5. Policies and procedures;

6. Communication style;

7. How much documentation of methodology is done and accepted; and

8. The personalities of the group members.

Individual Personalities and Skills

Politics, Power, and Group Interaction

Leading and managing the process of change is imperative in today's group practice, and in many ways is one of the most difficult tasks facing the medical practice executive. To paraphrase Darwin: survival goes to the most adaptable. Today, governance is not about the maintenance of the medical practice or the casual oversight of management, it is about the intense efforts to transform medical practices into effective health care delivery models that will thrive into the future. This requires governing bodies to be more than caretakers; they must exert active leadership. The board must be more than a collection of advocates for a cause. It must be a mission-driven body of individuals who bring different perspectives and talents to the meeting, but with a single purpose – to advance the mission of the group. Furthermore, the mission, goals, policies, procedures, and values of the organization have to be documented. In addition, every member of the organization should align behaviors to encourage adoption of these key success factors. This requires consistency, leadership, and above all, hard work and perseverance.

All of this makes governance one of the most significant issues for the medical group practice today. What makes a group practice a focused and effective organization has much more to do with how the governance structure is organized than it does with the practice's legal structure. As Exhibits 1 and 2 illustrate, the interaction of governance and operational activities is essential for the effective execution of the group's mission and to ensure, through monitoring those activities, that it will further the organization's mission.

Medical groups are traditionally viewed as professional collegial organizations. They have many unique features. Some of the features that affect governance are that the primary producers are all the owners (in many cases), the governed are also the governors (which leads to many policy quandaries), and the pervasive notion that one's particular view should be considered above all else. This proprietorship mentality leads to numerous issues for the governing body of the practice. Not unlike the U.S. government system, at some point the need to have continuity in governance and the

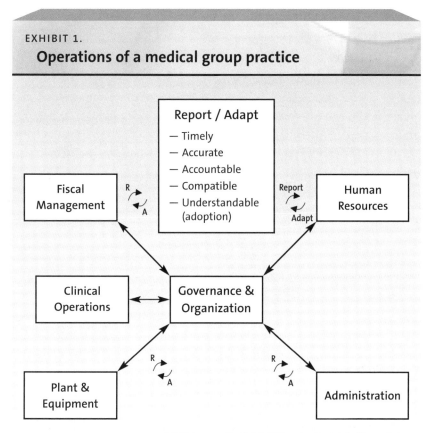

EXHIBIT 1.
Operations of a medical group practice

© 2005 Jones and Bartlett Publishers, Inc. Reprinted with permission.

need for more nimble business actions outweighs the need for a strict "one-person, one-vote" rule or the consensus approach that characterizes many group practice organizations.

This issue becomes more difficult, as well as more important, the larger and more diverse the group becomes. As groups grow, the need for a more centralized form of governance becomes important for many reasons:

- It becomes more difficult for members of the group to find time to participate. It also becomes more difficult to bring enough members of the group together to make policies and other decisions.

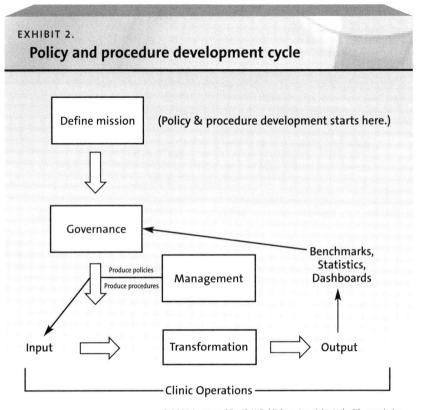

EXHIBIT 2.

Policy and procedure development cycle

Define mission   (Policy & procedure development starts here.)

Governance

Produce policies
Produce procedures

Management

Benchmarks,
Statistics,
Dashboards

Input   Transformation   Output

Clinic Operations

© 2005 Jones and Bartlett Publishers, Inc. Adapted with permission.

- Information disequilibrium increases. Some people are aware of and understand the issues, but some do not. This may be due to poor communication or to the lack of time to understand the issue or to become informed.

- The geographic limitations of attendance at meetings and other necessary absences from meetings make it difficult to deal with important issues.

- There is a general lack of interest in some topics needing discussion.

- The group members sense that they do not understand the issues or that their participation is not needed or welcomed.

"You cannot continually provide energy to a cause that you cannot champion, to a vision you can't share, to an organization you cannot believe in."[3] Medical groups must require more of their governance structure and go beyond micromanagement to leadership and transform their way of thinking. Transformational leadership requires a group change in thinking, a change in vocabulary, and shift of paradigms.

The medical practice executive must lead, not just manage. Management is focused on the maintenance of what "is." The medical practice executive must move to change the organization by leading and by creating the understanding that "what is" may not be in the best interest of the group or the individual in the future. The role of a manager is to help the members of the medical group understand what the possibilities are; the role of a leader is to help them embrace a compelling vision of the future. Groups must move from an ad hoc method of policy development and decision making to a more systematic process that allows for the coordination of governance and management.

Problem Solving, Decision-Making Patterns, Focus, and Follow-Through

Problem solving and decision making require inquiry. One of the major areas of concern in decision making involves the factors that prevent decisions from being made, sometimes referred to as "decision paralysis" factors. Five paralyses are detrimental to the process:

1. Resistance to change (paradigm paralysis);
2. Lack of communication (no collaboration among departments or within some departments);
3. Lack of written guidance (policies and procedures, or P&P)
4. Lack of employee empowerment; and
5. Lack of recognition of a need to change.

Many organizations fail to recognize the influence of "organizational culture" on the governance process within the entity. Governance flows from culture because the culture of the group will dictate how the group makes decisions.

■ The Decision-Making Process

The styles of decision making that naturally flow from the group's culture are:

- *Directive style* – typically adopted when tolerance for ambiguity is low and the decision makers tend to be uncompromising and rational in their thinking. Minimal information is used and few alternatives are given for consideration.

- *Analytical style* – typical when there is a higher tolerance for ambiguity and decision makers are rational in their thinking. Decision makers typically give careful consideration to unique situations.

- *Conceptual style* – seen when there is a high level of ambiguity and decision makers are intuitive rather than rational in their thinking.

- *Behavioral style* – seen when the decision maker wants to avoid conflict or places greater importance on social relationships and is receptive to suggestions.

Decision making has been studied in depth and can be divided into two types of problems: (1) well-structured/programmed problems, and (2) unstructured/unprogrammed problems. Structured problems involve goals that are clear and are often familiar because they have occurred before. Structured problems are easily and completely defined with available information. In addition, structured problems are usually programmed, are repetitive, and can be handled by a routine approach. Decision rules can be developed and applied over and over again. Such decisions can be easily delegated because the rules can be explained and assigned in advance, and do not need to involve the group's governance structure.

Types of programmed decisions involve:

- *Policy* – general guidelines for making a decision about a structural issue. An example is: "All employees receive 10 days of vacation after one year of service."

- *Procedure* – a series of interrelated steps that a manager can use to respond to a structure issue. For instance, a manager may calculate the amount of vacation an employee receives the same way each time.

- *Rules* – explicit statements that limit what can or cannot be done to carry out a procedure. For instance, a group could decide to prorate the amount of vacation for employees who do not work full time.

Change-Agent Management

As stated earlier, medical practice executives must lead, not just manage. Management and leadership are often confused with one another, however. Management's role is to implement the policies and execute the strategies determined by the governing body. The governing body will allocate resources for implementation, but it is the practice manager's responsibility to determine *how* the strategy is implemented. Implementation is not the function of the governing body, although this is frequently seen in the medical practice setting.

Members of the governing body must be leaders. To answer the question, "How do leaders lead?" consider some of the absolute requirements of leadership:

- *Interpret reality* in an understandable way.

- *Explain the present* in clear and factual terms.

- *Paint a picture of the future*, a compelling vision.

First, leaders must interpret reality in an understandable way. The current situation must be clear and unambiguous. This provides context for the actions needed to move the organization forward. Medical groups often are not fully aware of their current reality, or even how their surroundings (environment, patients, and the "outside" world) affect them, due to the lack of market surveillance with an eye to the future. They need to pulse the community.

This reality must be explained in ways that provide factual and therefore actionable information, free of the emotion and judgment that often clouds the picture and turns the focus to argument, not action. Once this basis is established for the present, a compelling picture can be developed for future action. After all, who would want to follow a leader who has little to offer in the future or little to say about that future? A big part of leadership is motivation to act. People have to believe in the vision of the future. They must want to see it happen. They must want to be part of that future.

Trust

An essential element for the governance of a medical practice is trust, partnered with its development and maintenance. Trust interrelationships within the medical group are numerous and interdependent, as shown in Exhibit 3.

A cornerstone in the readiness to change is trust; conversely, the failure to change is often due to a lack of trust. Trust comes in many flavors:

- *Authentic trust.* Trust between parties is earned over a period of time.

- *Naïve trust.* Trust is given without being earned – a sort of natural trust.

- *Blind trust.* Similar to naïve trust; trust is given because there is no reason *not* to trust the other party. Blind trust can be based on reputation or other factors.

The primary factor causing loss of trust is a sense of deception. It is essential in the medical group to preserve and, at times, regain trust by carefully communicating the following:

- Facts that have been carefully checked for accuracy;

- Admission of all mistakes (quickly); and

- Full disclosure of any given situation so that a lack of trust is not created due to a perception of providing "only part of the story."

Such communications should become a natural part of the interaction between group members.

EXHIBIT 3.

Trust interrelationships must be mediated by the governance process

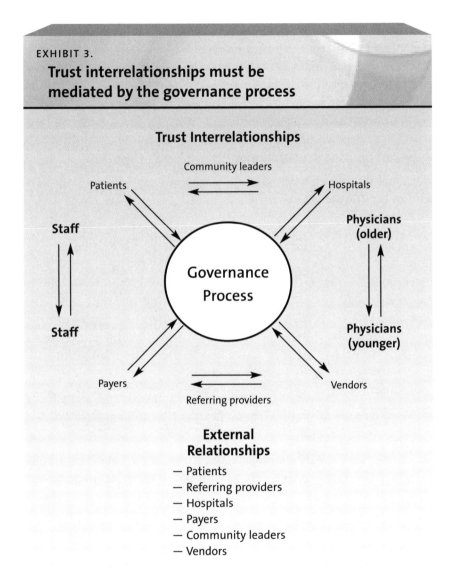

Trust Interrelationships

External
Relationships

— Patients
— Referring providers
— Hospitals
— Payers
— Community leaders
— Vendors

Negotiating and Implementing Change

Many medical group boards consist of all the physicians or all those physicians who have reached full shareholder or partnership status. Although this method may address the perennial question of autonomy and control, it does little to improve decision making or the speed at which decisions are made.

Many groups are beginning to address this issue. Where does the organization start? Understanding where the group is today is often a good way to decide where to go tomorrow. It is also wise to collect as much thoughtful opinion as possible. Surveying can be a useful – and powerful – tool. Exhibit 4 is a sample of a physician survey of the current situation for the Good Practice.

■ Performance Goals

The process of choosing goals has many aspects, from the informal to the formal analytical. Mintzberg's "Five Ps for Strategy"[4] and Porter's "Five Forces"[5] are excellent ways to work through the goal development and prioritization process, as well as to think about the many issues that are involved in looking at strategic goals. Although not all of the aspects of the Mintzberg and Porter models may be applicable in the group practice, the "Five Ps" and Porter's strategic framework may be translated to the following five considerations for developing sound group goals:

1. *Industry competitors.* A first step in the health care industry is to learn how medical many practices or services already exist in the market.

2. *Pressure from substitute products.* An example might be a family practice serving as a substitute for internal medicine or pediatrics.

3. *Bargaining power of suppliers.* Technology companies can often keep prices high and selectively discount prices only to the largest buyer, such as large healthcare systems.

4. *Bargaining power of buyers.* In health care, buyers, a.k.a. third-party payers, have significant bargaining power in large part because of the potential collective action by a group of patients through their carriers.

5. *Potential entrants.* What are the barriers for other medical practices and services entering the market? Barriers, such as

EXHIBIT 4.

Sample physician survey

At the physician retreat, we agreed to examine the issue of group governance for Good Practice. This survey is intended to provide input to the committee to help guide the process.

Please rate the following statements based on how strongly you agree or disagree with each of these issues in your association with Good Practice.

I. GOVERNANCE

	Strongly Agree				Strongly Disagree
1. The current governance practices of the clinic need to be changed.	5	4	3	2	1
2. I feel the Executive Committee could handle many issues without full board approval as long as I was kept informed of the process (e.g., last year's malpractice issue).	5	4	3	2	1
3. I feel the full board should meet less often.	5	4	3	2	1
4. I would be willing to allow a smaller group of physicians to make major clinical decisions so long as they are held accountable for their actions.	5	4	3	2	1
5. I would be willing to allow our clinic management greater autonomy in decision making for the clinic so long as they are held accountable for their actions.	5	4	3	2	1
6. We attend too many meetings on a regular basis.	5	4	3	2	1
7. There are too many physicians involved in the clinic decision-making processes.	5	4	3	2	1
8. The three divisions of the Good Practice should be more coordinated in terms of their decision making, not less.	5	4	3	2	1
9. I would be willing to have less personal autonomy to expedite decision making in the group.	5	4	3	2	1
10. I would be willing to devote significant time to the governance of the practice.	5	4	3	2	1

II. MISSION

1. The Good Practice should offer comprehensive care to the region even if that occasionally means investing in technologies or staffing that may not be profitable.	5	4	3	2	1
2. I would be willing to make less money to preserve lifestyle issues, such as time off.	5	4	3	2	1

recruiting, are the largest determinate of which practices or services might enter the market.

■ Meeting Management

One of the necessities of organizational governance and operations is the meeting. Meetings are very expensive because they take "billable" time away from the most economically valuable asset of the practice, the physicians. The medical practice executive should consider how much a group meeting will cost in lost productivity and use that as a benchmark to keep meeting times and numbers in check. Meetings are often seen as frequent time wasters, and it is the responsibility of the medical practice executive to recognize this perception and manage it carefully. Meeting management is a practiced art.

For meetings to be effective, they should have many of the following characteristics:

- *A clear task.* Is this an ad hoc or standing group? An *ad hoc* committee usually performs a specific task and may disband when the task is completed, whereas a *standing committee*, or a group such as the board, is often covered or mandated in the organization's bylaws. Any meeting body should have a clear expectation of its function and the time line, if necessary, to accomplish its task.

- *Participation.* Members who are selected to attend a meeting, either by appointment or election, should be committed to the group's work and tasks. Absent members can be disruptive because they will need to be brought up-to-date, and if they disagree with an outcome, work that was thought to be completed may have to be revisited.

- *Expectations.* Expectations should be realistic, and the meeting time should allow participation by all.

- *Rules* – Ground rules for behavior, discussion, and decorum should be established. The meeting should never turn into a hostile situation that might destroy relationships and the past good work of the meeting group. Meetings are rarely good places to resolve personal conflicts and disagreements, which should be taken "off-line."

- *Agenda.* The meetings themselves should have an agenda that is relevant to the governing body or committee meeting. Agendas should not include business related to other governing groups within the practice.

- *Schedule.* The meeting should start and stop on time, as established up front by the time frame indicated on the agenda. The meeting facilitator can show leadership by explaining the reason for hard start and stop times (e.g., respect for everyone's time). One of the greatest failures in managing meetings is an agenda that is too lengthy for the time allowed. The facilitator should assign times for each topic and stick to the times.

A "parking lot" approach will prevent alienating people and potentially losing good ideas. The parking lot is a simple but effective concept that, simply put, acknowledges an idea or topic as valid, but defers it to a future date or to a more appropriate body or person to handle, without taking excessive amounts of meeting time. Depending on the formality of the group, this information can be included in the minutes or simply written on a separate flip chart. The facilitator should follow up with regard to the parking lot issues. If the topic is appropriate for a future meeting, the facilitator should list it on a future agenda. If it is better addressed in another forum, then he or she should direct it there, with feedback to the committee members about the fate of the issue.

Recordkeeping

If careful records of meetings are not kept, several things will happen, none of which are good for the group. Without good minutes, the risk of losing valuable ideas and information about what took place at the meeting is significant. Errors will occur in communication with absent members or in recalling "what happened" at the last meeting. Different versions of the outcomes of many ideas and alternatives will undoubtedly emerge unless a record is kept. Such information, or misinformation, has the potential to spread to others in the group as well. The meeting's minutes are the vehicle for effectively communicating the results of the meeting. If more detail is necessary, an action plan that describes what steps will be taken to complete the activities that were the subject of the meeting is warranted.

Agenda

An example of a meeting agenda is shown below.

Agenda for the Board of Directors
ABC Medical Group
January 1, 2008

1. Call to Order	Chairperson	2 minutes
2. Minutes of the Previous Meeting	Approve	5 minutes
3. Business of the Meeting	Discuss and vote	60 minutes
4. Next Meeting	January 14, 2008	1 minute
5. Adjourn		

The important aspects of this agenda are the specification of the items to be addressed and their allotted times, as well as who is responsible for presenting the topic or what action is needed.

Facilitator

The facilitator, or chairperson, is in charge of the meeting. This means that he or she must keep the meeting on schedule, enforce the rules of decorum and order, use the parking lot approach, and actively seek participation from all members during discussion. The meeting's procedure should be clearly discussed in advance, and agreement needs to be obtained from the participants prior to the meeting.

For meetings to be effective, it is the chairperson's responsibility to watch out for the following adverse actions and to intercede if necessary:

- Personal attacks;

- A member appealing to his or her own expertise or expecting involvement when there is not any reason to do so. This is closely related to the personal attack because it indicts the expertise and work of the members or stakeholders presenting information or ideas and solutions;

- An appeal to popularity; this is very common;

- An appeal for pity (e.g., "poor me");

- A false dilemma, in which only two options to a problem are presented when, in fact, many more are available;

- A complex question for which several answers are required to properly respond, yet due to resource constraints, a variety of answers is rarely presented;

- A false analogy that compares two things that seem to be similar when they are not;

- A slippery slope, which is always very political (e.g., "If we give them a raise, they will expect a raise every year"); or

- An unrepresentative sample, which is a mainstay in rhetoric; a conclusion is drawn (or a decision is made) based on an anecdotal example.

■ Professional Standards

Written standards of conduct and expectations should be developed and implemented within every well-managed medical group. This forms the basis for what is expected of the group's members and is also essential for the continuation of group culture.

Professional Standards Committee

The professional standards committee consists of the department chiefs from each division (or, in smaller organizations, this might be the duty of the managing partner or senior partner). In addition, each department is required to have procedures in place to deal with performance and behavioral issues that do not merit escalation to the executive board level.

Professional Standards Document for Physicians

A professional standards document similar to the one presented here should be signed and become part of each physician's personnel file. A professional standards document for physicians could include the following expectations:

- Provide high-quality health services that respond to individual, family, and community needs;
- Maintain the integrity and quality of job performance by giving the best effort possible on the job;
- Provide health care services in compliance with all applicable laws, regulations, and standards, including state and federal legislation regarding patients' rights;
- Ensure each clinical assessment is undertaken by individuals qualified to conduct such assessment;
- Maintain medical records and documentation to meet the requirements of the medical staff bylaws, facilities policies, accreditation standards, and all applicable laws and regulations;
- Maintain medical records in a legible manner;
- Provide required documentation that the services were, in fact, provided. Use billing codes that accurately describe the services provided;
- Preserve the practice's property, facilities, equipment, and supplies – whether owned or leased;

- Encourage fellow physicians to develop their skills and potential;
- Actively strive to create a professional atmosphere that will be admired by physicians, patients, and visitors;
- Show respect and consideration for one another, regardless of position, station, or relationship;
- Recognize and support the diversity of the practice's physicians, staff, patients, and communities as a valuable asset;
- Use conflict resolution skills in managing disagreements;
- Address dissatisfaction with policies through appropriate channels;
- Communicate with others clearly and directly, displaying respect for their dignity;
- Address concerns about clinical judgment with associates directly and privately;
- Support policies promoting cooperation and teamwork;
- Address concerns about operational or physician performance issues in an appropriate setting and in a respectful manner;.
- Dress in a professional manner; and
- Disclose and avoid conflicts of interest.

Regarding the last expectation, conflicts of interest occur when a physician's outside interests or activities might compromise his or her obligations to patients or the practice. Due to the wide variety of activities that may constitute a conflict, a physician should consult the executive board if uncertain about a particular activity. If a conflict is identified, the preferred action is to terminate the outside activity or remove oneself from any activity in patient care or the practice that may constitute a conflict. If this is not possible, measures should be taken in consultation with the executive board to minimize the effects of such a conflict.

Unreasonable Behaviors

In general, an unreasonable behavior is any activity that undermines practice morale, heightens physician turnover, detracts from productive activities, increases the risk of ineffective or substandard practices, generates poor patient satisfaction, intimidates or threatens harm to others, or disproportionately causes distress to others in the work environment.

Unreasonable behavior includes, but certainly is not limited to, such behaviors as:

- Failing to comply with professional standards;

- Addressing nonconstructive criticism in such a way as to intimidate, undermine confidence, belittle, or to impute stupidity or incompetence;

- Imposing idiosyncratic requirements on nurses or other staff that do not add to quality patient care, but serve only to burden them with special treatment for the physician;

- Using foul or abusive language directed at staff or others associated with the practice, such as hospital personnel, vendors, and so on;

- Arbitrarily sidestepping policies;

- Acting in ways that could be perceived as sexual harassment;

- Criticizing staff in front of others;

- Showing disrespect or being discourteous;

- Relying on intimidation to get his or her way;

- Leveling attacks that are personal, irrelevant, or go beyond the bounds of fair, professional comments at others; respectful confrontations are helpful and encouraged, but personal attacks are out of bounds;

- Purposefully violating or ordering an employee to violate the practice's employment or physician policies;

- Retaliating in any way, at present or in the future, against any employee who reports an incident to the professional standards committee;

- Performing actions in the name of the group without the group's authorization; and

- Engaging in any other behavior, not specifically listed above, which, after report and investigation, is deemed disruptive by the professional standards committee.

Professional Standards Violation Policy for Physicians

The professional standards violation policy for physicians outlines collegial steps that can be taken in an attempt to resolve complaints about inappropriate conduct exhibited by physicians. There could, however, be a single incident of inappropriate conduct or a continuation of conduct that is so unacceptable as to make such collegial steps inappropriate. Therefore, nothing in this policy precludes immediate referral to the executive board, if warranted. It is the responsibility of the president or other physician leader of the medical group to refer the matter to the board.

The goal of this policy is to address and motivate a change in behavior that would be consistent with the professional standards, mission, vision, and core values established by the practice. Specifically, such a policy promotes collegial cooperation; recruitment and retention of quality physicians and staff; and incentives to achieve the practice's strategic goals.

If the professional standards committee receives a report of a second incident about a similar issue for the same physician within a two-year period and determines that inappropriate conduct has occurred, it may issue a report and recommendation to the executive board that could include a financial assessment. The recommended assessment amount should be determined by an average of the committee members' inputs through secret ballot, but should be within a predetermined upper and lower bound. This possible assessment would be deducted from the physician's paycheck on the payday following the executive board's approval.

If the committee receives a report of a third infraction of a similar nature, and if the committee determines that inappropriate conduct has occurred, the matter is then sent to the executive board for further action.

It is important to document a plan of correction that clearly addresses the desired improvement expected of the physician. This might include the following guidelines:

- Do not pass off work to other partners, either junior or senior, that you can or should do yourself;

- Provide comprehensive and careful patient care;

- Avoid comments to office staff that might have sexual connotations;

- Pay strict attention to patient confidentiality;

- Provide sole call coverage. Only rarely should a call be made to partners at home regarding patients when these physicians are not on call;

- Avoid confrontational behavior with others in the office and hospital;

- Avoid doing "accounting" of procedures (e.g., who has done the most or least procedures or patient visits);

- Be courteous on the telephone and to all staff, physicians, and partners at any location; and

- Be a team player. Be punctual and do not leave before the normal work day is over without checking with partners to see if all work is completed.

TASK 2 **Construct and Maintain Governance Systems**

THE GROUP'S GOVERNANCE begins with a clear understanding of what the process of governance entails and what the role of governance is or should be in the practice.

■ Strategic Planning Process

One of the most important, but often most neglected, aspects of a group practice organization is a clear mission statement that is consistent with the values of the organization's members. The successful organization must develop its mission as a guide to all of the group's activities (see Exhibit 5).

A mission and values statement for a medical group should be similar to the example shown here.

Mission: The ABC Medical Group will provide care of the highest quality to our patients within an environment that is compassionate, ethical, and economically sound. We will accomplish this by:

1. Always putting patients first; maintaining clinical excellence; and seeking to improve care through research, system enhancement, innovation, and continuing education.

EXHIBIT 5.

Physician mission guides group activities

2. Being ethical in all of our dealings with patients, colleagues, employees, our hospitals, third-party payers, vendors, and our community.

3. Providing value to our patients, insurance carriers, and hospitals, and being seen as an asset to our community.

4. Having an effective organization that provides quality care, efficient service, effective communication, cost-effective treatment, and a competent and positive workforce.

5. Recognizing the value of the group – that the group is greater than the sum of its members.

6.   Being focused on the creation of a positive environment that shows compassion and caring for our patients and our staff members.

7.   Providing attractive salary and benefits packages that are competitive with all national standards, allowing the ABC Medical Group to attract and keep the most talented physicians and employees.

The mission of the medical group needs to be reviewed and considered on a regular basis. Consider what has changed about the group. Is the group living up to the mission it has set for itself? Or is the mission statement simply a wall decoration, with little relationship to what the group believes is important and what it does?

An essential element of group planning and strategic activity is the board retreat (see Task 3). This event should combine educational time, with internal and external speakers, with time to consider issues that are of strategic interest to the group. These issues are often related to:

- Growth;
- Competition;
- Changes in services or development of new services;
- Examination of future scenarios, how they will play out, and what their effect may be on the group; and
- Re-examination (or development) of a mission statement.

■ Analysis of the Medical Practice

Cost/Benefit Analysis

A number of methods to analyze costs, benefits, and risks are associated with any decision or plan. The procedure, however, will always involve the following steps:

1. Define the plan or the decision and the process by drawing a flowchart or list of all inputs, outputs, activities, and events;

Use the budget or other financial statements and information as guides;

2. Calculate the cost and benefit of each service (include, if possible, direct, indirect, financial, and social costs and benefits); and

3. Compare the sum of the costs with the sum of the benefits.

4. Select the best choices if alternatives are being considered.

Risk can be considered by evaluating the likelihood of failure and assigning a weight to each alternative that has been identified in the analysis. By determining weighted average likelihood of success or failure for each alternative, a risk stratification of the alternatives is possible. For example, there are five alternatives, and the likelihood of failure is 10, 12, 30, 40, and 50 percent, respectively. Clearly, the first alternative has the greatest chance of success, and this information can be incorporated into the discussion.

Group Self-Assessment

Assessing service quality and patient outcomes is becoming essential to the modern medical group practice. The medical group's customers (patients and their families) have ever-increasing expectations of medical services, which have a direct correlation to the group's strategic and operational plans.

Michael Porter writes extensively about group competitiveness and has outlined three fundamental operational strategies:[6]

- Focus
- Differentiation
- Price

In a medical practice, *focus* takes shape as a specialty focus or a service-line focus. Quality in services that meet or exceed customer expectations is a key *differentiator* for medical groups. There is little opportunity to deal with *pricing* issues in many medical practice settings. The presentation of these data by administration or committees to the board is essential.

Practices need their patients to be advocates for them in the marketplace. It has been said that "if we take care of the patients, they will take care of us." That becomes especially important as pay for performance and other stringent standards are introduced by the market. Pay for performance is a new element that integrates quality and customer issues into pricing strategies for many of the health care organizations' largest payers, including (but not limited to) companies such as Medicare, United HealthCare, and Aetna. Technical quality simply is no longer sufficient. It is necessary and required to provide technically competent service, but insufficient alone for the future medical group to be successful. Patient satisfaction is a key element, as value is established as a function of price and quality. Quality is an aggregate measure of patient satisfaction, technical competence, and medical quality.

SWOT Analysis

One of the most widely used methods for strategic planning is the analysis of Strengths, Weaknesses, Opportunities, and Threats, or a "SWOT" analysis (see Exhibit 6). The SWOT process involves sev-

EXHIBIT 6.
SWOT analysis

INTERNAL CAPABILITIES	EXTERNAL ENVIRONMENT
Strengths	**Opportunities**
What does your practice do well?	*Where are the opportunities for your practice?*
Weaknesses	**Threats**
What part of your practice needs improvement?	*What is happening in your area that could threaten your practice?*

eral steps and is often done in the context of a group meeting or retreat.

A SWOT analysis helps to find the best match between external environmental trends (opportunities and threats) and internal capabilities (strengths and weaknesses). Specifically,

- A *strength* is a resource or capacity the organization can use effectively to achieve its objectives.

- A *weakness* is a limitation, fault, or defect in the organization that will keep it from achieving its objectives.

- An *opportunity* is any favorable situation in the organization's environment. It is usually a trend or change of some kind or an overlooked need that increases demand for a product or service and permits the firm to enhance its position by supplying it.

- A *threat* is any unfavorable situation in the organization's environment that is potentially damaging to its strategy. The threat may be a barrier, a constraint, or anything external that might cause problems, damage, or injury.

■ Organizational Communication Pathways

Communication pathways may be formal or informal, as well as positive or negative, in terms of accuracy and organizational impact. The pathway needs to fit the purpose of the communication and should be determined by the content to be presented. For example, one would not "fire" an employee in front of a large public group; likewise, one would not announce a new service to one person at a time through private meetings. As a general rule, the more complex the message, the greater the need for high-involvement communications – smaller, more structured, with more documentation and follow-up. The complexity might be defined by the nature of the communication or its impact on the community or the group.

Good communications always require careful planning, appropriate channel selection, and a consistent, professional message. Repetition and reinforcement of the message are also keys to having the audience "receive" and "remember" the intended message. Among the many diverse channels for communicating a group's message are:

Formal channels:

- Memos
- E-mail
- Documents, such as letters
- Meetings, small or large (private or public)
- Newsletters
- Mass media

Informal channels:

- E-mail
- Mass media
- Word of mouth
- Rumor mill
- Informal meetings

E-mail and mass media can be both formal and informal. Mass media can be directed to individual groups as well as other groups on a more informal indirect basis. E-mail can be sent to an individual or a few individuals in a rather informal way or used to broadcast important policy or procedure changes and updates to the group at large.

■ Teaming Principles

The roles of physician and nonphysician leadership within the medical group will vary greatly from group to group, but certain principles will, or should, apply, regardless of the size or structure of the group. The best model is the physician/administrator executive team, in which a physician and practice executive work collaboratively to provide leadership to the group.

The tasks for the members of this type of team may be very similar and include:

- Development of policies, plans, and procedures;
- Licensing, compliance, and continued training;
- Quality assurance, monitoring, and organizational performance;
- Advisory role to the governing board;
- Staff development planning;
- Liaison for professional and nonprofessional staff;
- Interaction with patients, complaint resolution, and service recovery; and
- Interaction with outside groups and organizations.

How tasks are carried out and which leader performs each task will depend on how much time the physicians have for these duties, as well as their skill sets, experience, and attitude about the work.

Many groups do provide some so-called "administrative" time to physician leaders, and some large practices have full-time medical directors, but in most smaller groups, leadership and governance are voluntary activities or may even be assigned by the group.

Groups may have "rotating" physician leadership, which is intended to spread the responsibility in an egalitarian manner throughout the group. Such a plan, however, ignores the reality that leadership and effective governance are skills that must be learned, nurtured and developed. Such an ad hoc approach does not consider the aptitude of leaders to lead. Some people are better leaders than others. The same can be said for the administrative staff. However, a trained administrator should be able to address a wide range of problems and issues facing the governance and organizational dynamics of the group.

Relationship building is fundamental to the successful team. In his book *The Five Dysfunctions of a Team*,[7] Patrick Lencioni talks about five clear and easily identifiable factors that prevent effective teamwork, be it a 2- or 20-person team:

1. Lack of trust;
2. Fear of conflict;

3. Lack of commitment;

4. Avoidance of accountability; and

5. Inattention to results.

A great team's members are business partners. They trust one another, communicate openly, and keep the best interests of the group in mind with all decisions. Above all, they offer each other respect and unconditional support. Someone who cannot support the team in an unconditional way needs to resign from the team, resolve the conflict behind closed doors, or accept a poorly performing team. The typical advocacy form of interaction is passé and useless for the transformation and development of the group; it only achieves the goals of one individual or a small group of individuals.

Team leadership can best be told with the story of the buffalo and the geese. Buffalo Bill discovered early in his legendary slaughter of these great beasts that he could effectively kill an entire herd by first shooting the lead bull. Once the lead bull dropped, the other animals became confused and in fact they would stop, not knowing what to do, thereby becoming easy targets for the sharpshooters.

In contrast, a flock of geese flies in a "V" shape, not due to an artistic flare, but because it is efficient. By flying behind one another in formation, wind resistance is reduced and the most distance is then covered with the least expenditure of energy. Of course, the lead goose is blazing the trail and eventually will get tired and drop back in the "V" – only to be replaced by another goose. This is a trait that any organization should strive to emulate. If one goose gets sick, they will all land, and another goose will accompany the sick goose until it dies or is well enough to proceed. Geese also honk, not to telegraph their location, but to encourage the goose in front of them to keep flying and to tell their leader, "we are behind you!"[8]

Committee Structures

An essential element of governance is the delegation of task and duties for the group. The principal governing body may decide, as allowed or even required by the group's bylaws, to develop a committee structure that addresses operational concerns and process within the group in conjunction with the administration. This is a great way to provide physician input in a structured, instead of an ad hoc, way. It also provides a great opportunity to develop future leaders by educating them in the committee process and its importance to the business of the group and the issues that face the modern medical group.

Some of the more common committees within the governance structure are:

- Finance;
- Personnel;
- Technology;
- Quality review;
- Management (usually smaller groups);
- Research;
- Recruiting;
- Education;
- Managed care;
- Practice development;
- Performance; and
- Ad hoc committees for many purposes, such as strategic planning, new building, service-line development, and contract review.

Focus of Group Activities

Governing also needs to be concerned with the focus of group activities. Activities need to be grouped with consideration for function and customer interaction. In addition, leadership must be empowered to implement and act upon the governing board's policies and decisions. Typically this would mean the group should focus on three areas, as shown in Exhibit 7:

1. Internal functions;

2. External functions; and

3. Operations.

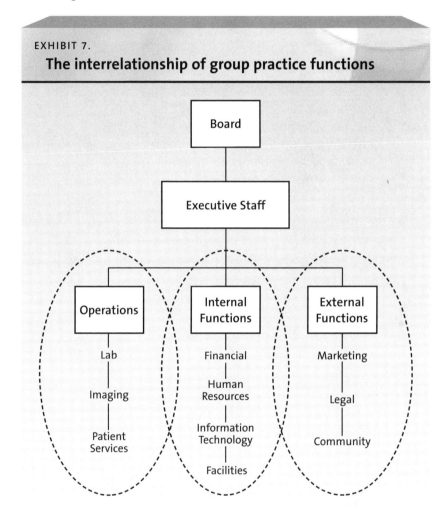

EXHIBIT 7.

The interrelationship of group practice functions

Regular reports to the board, as well as benchmarking these activities, can be very useful for the effective governance of the organization. It is also important to understand the nature of the interaction of these focal lines of activities. This interaction has to be governed carefully to prevent a "silo" mind-set or "group think" from emerging.

■ Governance Legal Structures

Business enterprises, including health care providers, use a variety of organizational forms as the legal structure for their activities. Their choice is based on how an entity provides legal and tax advantages and liability protection, and how it fits with the practice's overall business and professional goals.

It is important to understand the legal structures of the medical practice, especially in terms of liability and taxation issues. Most medical groups in the United States take one of the following legal forms:

- Sole proprietorship/solo practice (with no separate legal entity);
- Professional corporation (PC) or professional association (PA);
- Professional limited liability partnership (PLLP);
- Professional limited liability company (PLLC);
- Business corporation, either for-profit or nonprofit; or
- General partnership.

State laws dealing with corporations and other forms of legal entities define the benefits and requirements of each of these structures. Medical practices are typically organized and operated through the use of a separate legal entity (e.g., a separately incorporated professional corporation) in order to shield the practice's owners' assets from any of the liabilities of the practice. This shield of "limited liability" is available, to differing degrees, under state laws allowing for the creation and use of PCs, PLLCs, and PLLPs. Few medical practices use a general partnership or limited partnership form of organization, primarily because these legal forms do not provide the shield of limited liability available through other forms.

From a tax perspective, the federal internal revenue code and the Internal Revenue Service (IRS) also define how each of these legal structures will be treated. For example, the IRS allows professional corporations to be taxed the same as any other corporation (via "C" corporation tax treatment). Some professional corporations with only a limited number of members can select an "S" corporation status, which enables the entity to be taxed as a partnership.

Physicians are always encouraged to seek legal advice prior to selecting a particular form of business entity to be used for a medical practice. An attorney (as well as an accountant) should be consulted before deciding which form of entity to choose. Different legal forms have different benefits and burdens, and the best choice will depend on the practice's circumstances and goals. For example, most medical practices today use the PC form of entity, although an increasing number of practices are using a PLLC or PLLP form.

Key to Choosing an Attorney

When choosing legal counsel, physicians typically select a firm experienced in working with medical groups. Other physicians and the county medical society can provide recommendations.

Sole Proprietorship

A sole proprietorship is a business with a single owner, but not established as a separate entity. In such a structure, the assets of the individual physician and the medical practice are not separate, so the physician does not benefit from the shield of limited liability provided by a PC or similar form.

Some solo practices are organized in the form of PCs or similar legal entities that are owned by a single physician. Under such a structure, the physician is able to work in a solo practice format while also obtaining the benefits of the shield of limited liability that are offered by the use of the corporate form.

Advantages:

- *Control and flexibility.* The physician-owner has total control over money and decisions because there are no partners or shareholders.

- *Ease*. A sole proprietorship is relatively easy to set up and requires no separate tax filing.

Disadvantages:

- *No history*. It can sometimes be difficult for a new practice to borrow funds if it has no collateral.

- *No backup*. No one else can see patients when the sole proprietor is on vacation or is incapacitated for any reason – the cash flow simply stops.

- *Full liability*. In a true sole proprietorship, the physician-owner – not a separate legal entity – is responsible for all liabilities of the practice.

- *Full responsibility*. The physician-owner is responsible for all decisions.

Professional and Business Corporations

A professional corporation is a legal entity that is separate from its owners. Some states call this same form a professional association, or a service corporation (SC). A PC has four characteristics:

1. Limited liability;

2. Continuity of existence;

3. Transferability of ownership; and

4. Centralized management.

The PC is viewed as a separate entity for both liability and taxation purposes. A PC is generally subject to the same basic requirements and rules as any other business corporation, except that the "professional" corporation variant requires that only licensed professionals (e.g., physicians) may own an interest in the practice. This means, for example, that a nonphysician generally cannot be an investor in a physician's PC. Additionally, ownership can be transferred only to another licensed professional.

Similar to a PC, a business corporation is also a separate legal entity that limits the liability of its owners. A business corporation, however, allows for outside investors. This form of legal entity allows ownership by nonphysician investors. Use of a business corporation is common for general commercial business activities, but such a form is rarely used for medical practices because most state licensing laws require that only physicians can own interests in a medical practice.

Advantages:

- *Limited liability.* Shareholders or owners are not liable for the debts of the practice.
- *Tax deductions.* Because the corporation pays the benefits, items such as health and life insurance become tax-deductible expenses of the corporation.
- *Transferability.* Ownership is transferable to another licensed person or entity.

Disadvantages:

- *Profits taxed.* Corporate-retained earnings are taxed, although this can be avoided in many instances by selecting "S" corporation treatment for tax purposes.
- *Governance.* The legal form of a corporation requires a governance structure with a board and elected officers.

Professional Limited Liability Partnerships and Professional Limited Liability Companies

Both a PLLP and a PLLC provide different levels of legal protection or limited liability to the organization's owners. Both legal forms allow the profits from the partnership or LLC to be taxed as partnerships – meaning that there is no potential for "double taxation" of entity profits, as in the case of a corporate form.

Like corporations, under most state laws LLCs and LLPs must be organized as "professional" versions of these legal forms. Ownership in the practices is restricted to licensed physicians. The procedure for setting up these or other forms of organizations is defined by state law, although most require filing articles of organization or similar documents with the state.

Advantage of both structures:

- *Limited personal liability*. The practice is treated as a partnership for tax purposes, so income and losses are passed through to the owners and not subject to double taxation.

Disadvantages of both structures:

- *Governance*. It is more difficult to establish strong governance.
- *Not employees*. Physicians generally are not employees of PLLPs or PLLCs, so they usually are not entitled to the same benefits as found in a PC or similar format.
- *Different financial management*. Both entities require financial management practices somewhat different from those found in the more common PC form.
- *Variable state laws*. Not every state allows the creation or use of a PLLP or PLLC for medical practices.

Summary

Few medical practices will use a general partnership or a limited partnership form of organization, primarily because the legal form does not provide the shield of limited liability available through other forms. Medical practices should always consult with an attorney well versed in health care law before deciding upon a particular form of legal entity and associated tax treatment.

■ Conclusions

One question that always needs to be answered when considering practice structure is the influence of form on the culture of the group and the governance system that a group envisions. In other words, the governance structure of a group will affect the culture, which will ultimately influence the operational nature of the group. For example, if there is not a centralized governance system and the culture of the group is biased toward significant physician autonomy, then operational operations will likely be variable, with standardization lacking.

TASK 3 # Evaluate and Improve Governing Bylaws, Policies, and Processes

■ Board of Directors

There is widespread agreement that the principal roles of the board are to:

- Develop the organizational mission;
- Provide and monitor institutional goals;
- Hire, evaluate, compensate, and interact with the chief executive officer (CEO);
- Take responsibility for and ensure the quality of care;
- Deal with external constituents (media, community, and government);
- Monitor the organization;
- Do the planning (financial and other); and
- Evaluate its own performance as a governing body.

In medical groups, most members of the board are physicians; although their duty is to the group as a whole, they may find it difficult from time to time to let their own interests or the interests of their specialty take a back seat for the good of the whole.

Board Composition and Meeting Procedural Rules

Most times, board membership occurs via an election, and those election rules will be specified in the bylaws of the organization. It is imperative that the group's bylaws be properly adopted and that the procedures outlined in the bylaws are adhered to carefully. Failure to correctly follow the process could result in a challenge to the legitimacy of the process and invalidate actions under state law.

Board Evaluation

The board's prospective members need to be evaluated based upon their performance of predetermined criteria that have been communicated clearly before an individual becomes a member of the board.

In addition, on an annual basis (at least), the board should conduct a useful self-review of performance and provide feedback to the individual board members. This should include a checklist of board responsibilities. Evaluation of present board members could include:

1. Board members must meet the attendance requirement. This is usually a high percentage of all meetings, often 75 percent.

2. Board members must come prepared to meet and discuss the agenda items.

3. What expertise is each specific member asked to contribute? Is the member an expert in business operations? finance? marketing? legal? It is not uncommon for the group's legal counsel to attend board meetings. At least in theory, board meetings can be protected by attorney/client privilege when legal counsel is present.

4. Board members must respect the confidentiality of the board's activities. They must also respect the decisions of the board outside the boardroom.

5. Board members must disclose conflicts of interest.

6. Board members must show respect to management and its role to implement board policy.

7. Board members must act in a prudent manner and understand that their behavior is representative of the group at all times.

Response to Stakeholders' Needs

The medical group's board must deal with a number of stakeholders in the quest to provide effective governance of the group. Some of these stakeholders are:

- Physicians in the practice;
- Other physicians in the community;
- Employees;
- Patients and their families;
- Payers;
- Government agencies – federal, state, and local;
- The community at large; and
- Hospitals.

Role of the Board

The role of the board should be clearly understood. The responsibility of the board is mostly about relationship management, but there are some specific tasks involved with each board member's role, including:

1. Relationship management with the administrator of the group;
2. Goal setting;
3. Interaction with other leaders in the group;
4. Relationship management with the group's constituencies;
5. Quality control and assessment;
6. Financial concerns – keeping a health group fiscally sound;
7. Self-assessment and development;

8. Performance monitoring; and

9. Mission focus.

It is very important that every potential member of the board understand his or her role and the expectations of the job. For example, a prospective board member might read a job description similar to the following sample:

The ABC Medical Practice's Board Member
Job Description and Expectations

Purpose	To advise, govern, oversee policy and direction, and to assist with the leadership and general promotion of the practice so as to support the organization's mission and needs and to work closely with the administration of the practice in order to achieve its goals.
Number of Members	[Specify the number of members. The typical number is between 5 and 11, depending on the size of the group.]
Major Responsibilities	– Organizational leadership and advisement – Organization of the executive committee officers and committees – Formulation oversight of policies and procedures – Financial management [to be defined] – Review and adopt budget for the organization; review quarterly financial reports; assist administration with budgetary issues as necessary – Oversight of program planning and evaluation – Hiring, evaluation, and compensation of senior administrative staff – Review of organizational and programmatic reports – Promotion of the organization – Strategic planning and implementation
Length of Term	[Specify length of term, which may be staggered.]
Meetings & Time Commitment	[Specify the time and location of meetings such as, "The executive committee will meet every other Friday commencing at 7:30 a.m., and meetings will

typically last one (1) hour (this may need to be revised)." An alternative would be to have monthly meetings (2 to 3 hours) in the afternoon or evening (consider payment to participants).]

Expectation of
Board Members
- Attend and participate in meetings on a regular basis and special events as possible.
- Participate in standing committees of the board and serve on ad hoc committees as necessary.
- Help communicate and promote mission and programs of the practice.
- Become familiar with the finances and resources of the practice as well as financial and resource needs.
- Understand the policies and procedures of the practice.

Board and Committee Structure

Establishing Committees
It shall be the responsibility of the executive committee to establish ad hoc and permanent standing committees as necessary to assist in the functioning of the practice. Whenever possible, these committees should contain a representative of the executive committee to provide a proper liaison as well as an administrative staff person.

Typical Committees
[Include: finance, personnel, marketing, quality care, and technology. In areas where managed care risk contracting is a significant part of the business environment, a utilization management committee would be common to oversee the risk management of these contracts.]

Board Meeting Management

Most board meetings are governed by Robert's Rules of Order,[9] which is the most widely accepted set of procedures for conducting business. These rules are extensive and cover a number of procedures that apply to the medical group setting. Some, however, may not apply to every group's needs, although familiarity with Robert's as a whole is important.

Outside Board Members

Increasingly, medical groups are beginning to behave more like traditional business corporations. As part of this change, groups are adding outside persons to the board to improve the governance process and to bring in new ideas and perspectives. These individuals must be chosen carefully with consideration of a number of important criteria.

Examples of these selection criteria for the practice's outside board member include:

- A general understanding of the region, its business climate, political environment, and some of the key community drivers, as well as some perspective on health care and what is happening in the broad view;

- A strategic thinker;

- Willing and able to attend meetings;

- Able to treat information discreetly;

- Some experience as a member of a board;

- No conflicts of interest or the appearance of such conflicts (e.g., not someone looking to do business with the clinic);

- General business acumen;

- A contributor who will not dominate the board;

- A history of working well in a group setting – a good fit;

- Willingness to sign a confidentiality agreement; and

- Willingness to accept fair compensation.

■ Bylaws

Like policies and procedures, bylaws are dynamic documents that require maintenance on a regular basis. Changes in corporate law may require amendments to the bylaws, so a general review of corporate documents should be completed at least annually with special attention being paid to those areas that may have been the subject of changes during the year.

The following questions should be considered as the bylaws and policies of the group are reviewed:

1. Has the group changed any committees this year?

2. Has the group changed any of its procedures on elections?

3. Has the group added any new shareholders or have any departed? If so, was their stock exchanged according to the bylaws?

4. Do key decisions fit the duties outlined for officers and directors?

5. Are minutes of meetings recorded and was a quorum present when decisions were made?

6. Does the group do things differently today than it did in the past?

7. Has state corporate law changed since the group's bylaws were last reviewed by legal counsel?

Administrators must protect the integrity of the bylaws because failure to act within the scope of the bylaws many cause legal action by aggrieved shareholders and unnecessary intergroup relationship concerns. It is wise to periodically review the requirements of the bylaws with the board so the board members fully understand their requirements. It is essential that new board members be oriented to and understand this material.

■ Organizational History

Organizational culture is an extremely important aspect of practice governance. Of course, positive cultures need to be maintained, and any negative culture needs to become a more positive one. Culture can be maintained by a focus on those aspects that are desirable. Recording the history of the group can enhance positive culture maintenance and make its accomplishments known. Publishing the history of the group and its culture in newsletters and Websites is important.

Cultural icons, such as photographs, awards, news articles, and mementos that are symbolic of important events in the group's history, should be properly archived and/or displayed. Activities such as service awards emphasize the group's positive values, which reinforces the importance of such ideals to new employees and physicians.

By its very nature, tribal knowledge is passed between stakeholders by storytelling and relaying the group's mythology to younger members. This information points to what is meaningful to its members, not necessarily to archivists. Be careful to identify and remember the stories that roam the hallways, because an unconscious amount of value may be placed on these traditions and attributes that we celebrate and share – and it needs to be recognized and remembered.

■ Recordkeeping

Record retention is a critical issue in group practices. There are several medical practice concerns as well as legal issues to consider when retaining records. Laws regarding recordkeeping vary from state to state. Policies need to be developed to clearly indicate:

- Type of record: financial, employee, property, tax returns, medical record, or other;
- Whether electronic or paper;
- Location of the record;
- How long it should be retained;
- Who is authorized to order record destruction; and
- Who should have access to records.

Record-retention policies should be reviewed at least annually to update and consider issues related to compliance.

■ Surveys

Survey Techniques

It can be difficult to obtain accurate customer information. Medical group practices can access general patient data in publicly available survey results (e.g., journals; newspapers; professional associations such as MGMA, the American Hospital Association, or the American Medical Association; and the government). Many practices, however, will find it necessary to go directly to their own patients to get the information they need.

There are various ways in which a practice might go about finding this information:

- Telephone interviews;
- Face-to-face interviews;
- Mail survey questionnaires;[10]
- On-site survey questionnaires;[11] and
- Customer complaint data from interviews and questionnaires.

Survey Tools

Of the many considerations when designing an interview or survey tool, the following are particularly important:

- Interviews or surveys should be constructed carefully, with attention paid to both the comprehensiveness of the questions and their usefulness. There is no point in asking a question if no action can result from its answer!

- Surveys should not alienate the customer. Filling in questionnaires and being interviewed takes valuable time – what's in it for them?

- The right individuals should be targeted. If the customer is a company rather than an individual, whose answers are you actually going to get?

- Resources should be set aside to prepare as well as run surveys or interviews, and also to collate and interpret the results.

■ Who will act on the results? What will they do?

Once the data have been collected, it is necessary to analyze them to get useful information for decision making and planning. Statistics is a process of making generalizations about a data set, based on data gathered from a smaller subset of the universe of events or by sampling. Statistical significance is achieved when the results (e.g., the difference in the mean scores of two groups) are larger than expected based just on random variation, also known as statistical "noise." Probability theory indicates how great a difference is needed to determine that the result is a real difference between the two data sets, known generally as statistical significance.

There are two key concepts in determining statistical significance:[12]

■ Distribution of a variable; and

■ Sampling distribution of means, or a list of all the averages for all the groups of data.

Statistics can be developed to help the organization make decisions about these data. These statistics will include averages (e.g., average age of the practice's patients, average charge per patient, average number of visits each year). Such statistical data always offers certainty in answering questions during the planning processes and the ability to compare the practice's data with those of other practices. SPSS (Statistical Package for the Social Sciences)[13] is an excellent statistical program that allows this process to be automated. It handles very large databases with ease.

Once the survey results have arrived and have been tallied and analyzed, the group must decide how to act on these results. Implement a new program or ancillary service? Institute a new way of billing or patient flow? Establish a customer service policy? Add a new payer or hospital to the plan? Many new revenue streams may be realized by listening to stakeholders. Taking a risk is important when stakeholders are telling your group about deficiencies. The next step is feasibility planning and fitting it to the operational plan. (Also refer to Task 1.)

TASK 4 **Conduct Stakeholder Needs Assessment and Facilitate Relationship Development**

■ Organizational Constituents and Needs

Through administration and executive function, the governing body is responsible for two activities that are essential to understanding the needs of stakeholders. The first is to communicate and commiserate by monitoring and collecting information. The *CLLASS* system is a good method to do this.

C – Contact constituents and use a variation of the MBWA (managing by walking around) approach.

L – Look around – what looks right and what doesn't?

L – Listen to what people are saying and not saying as well as what can be heard without asking a question.

A – Assimilate this information and look for trends or patterns.

S – Seek out people who are known to hold insight into the group's culture and function.

S – Speak out to the governing bodies in the group about this information on a regular basis.

Next, it is helpful at times to use the *SOC* method with the group.

S – Survey.

O – Operationalize the survey into plans of action.

C – Cycle – do it on a regular basis.

■ Surveys

General surveying should be simple, frequent, and receive attention. Examples of useful surveys are:

- Employee satisfaction;
- Morale;
- Customer and patient satisfaction;
- Physician satisfaction and attitude; and
- Referring-physician satisfaction.

Surveys can often be extremely simple. For example, a morale survey might consist of one question rated on a scale of 1 to 5: "What is your morale or the morale of your department?" Every negative response should raise a red flag for further evaluation and follow-up.

Survey tools and techniques are addressed in this volume's Task 3.

■ Needs Assessment Methodologies

Medical practices are dependent on and essential to the community where they are located. Assessing the needs and the assets of the community is an important way to conduct a complete analysis of any strategic scenario. Community information is essential in determining the need for:

- Additional providers;
- Specialties or ancillary services needed;
- Economic trends;
- Employment rates; and

- Growth and age distribution.

Fortunately, a great deal of information for community assessment is available so that the practice executive does not need to independently collect such data. Some of these sources are shown in Exhibit 8. Other sources include directories or inventories of

EXHIBIT 8.

Sources for community assessment information

Information	Sources

Economic data	U.S. Census Bureau, www.census.gov/
	Bureau of Labor Statistics – 202-691-5200,
	  www.bls.gov/
	U.S. Department of Housing and Urban
	  Development – 202-708-1112, www.hud.gov/
	Annual reports prepared by cities, counties,
	  and states

Public health data and vital statistics	State and local departments of health and human services

Education data	U.S. Department of Education – 1-800-USA-LEARN,
	  www.ed.gov
	The National Center for Education Statistics –
	  202-502-7300, http://nces.ed.gov/
	State and local education agencies

Child welfare	Human service departments

Information on children and youth	*Kids Count* data books published by the Annie E.
	  Casey Foundation – 410-547-6600,
	  www.aecf.org/
	The Children's Defense Fund – 1-800-233-1200,
	  www.childrensdefense.org/
	The National Center for Children in Poverty –
	  646-284-9600, www.nccp.org/

Health care data	Department of Health and Human Services
	  for the state
	Medicare, Centers for Medicare & Medicaid
	  Services – 877-267-2323, www.cms.hhs.gov
	Health plans
	Employers

agencies, surveys of practitioners, surveys of community-based organizations, telephone directories, agencies and organizations, and nonprofit and service organizations. It is also important to be represented in community development organizations such as the chamber of commerce and to regularly attend meetings.

■ Program Development

It is easy for a group practice to have an inaccurate view about the perspective of the community or any constituency. Organizing a focus group is an excellent way to collect important information about these potential markets. This technique is often superior to surveying because one is able to follow up questions with additional probing questions when there is a need to clarify an answer or when surprising information is revealed and requires further exploration.

Focus groups are structured, moderated discussions that bring together small groups of people in neutral settings to talk about issues related to the group practice. Discussion is a powerful means of learning from patients, community members, employees, physicians from the practice, referral physicians, and other stakeholders about their perceptions, experiences, values, and beliefs. It is also a good way to encourage community involvement or the involvement of anyone who may not otherwise have direct access to the governing or administrative processes in the group. When outside people are asked to participate, they frequently are surprised that their input is desired and valued. The act of conducting a focus group is appreciated.

The following guidelines can help a medical group practice create a useful focus group:

- Include all relevant age groups;

- Ensure that group members reflect the ethnic, linguistic, economic, and cultural diversity of the community;

- Conduct several sessions on different dates and at different times to ensure broad participation; and

- Control those who might overtalk, overshadow, or interrupt those who might be less vocal.

An impartial facilitator is best to guide discussion. The facilitator should keep conversation flowing and focused and should not dominate any discussion.

Focus groups are a great way for internal and external stakeholders to communicate and get to know one another's goals, ideals, and frustrations. This is particularly important for internal stakeholders (e.g., staff, physicians, leadership) because employees from a group sometimes forget the bigger picture of satisfied customers – patients, payers, and the community at large.

TASK 5 **Facilitate Staff Development and Teaming**

■ Staff Development Techniques

The interactions of the group's physicians are an area of great concern for most organizations. It is important that physicians understand their role in the organization, the culture of the organization ("how we do things"), and what is expected of them individually as well as in a group. Effective management of these relationships will help to ensure that new physicians are successful in their practices and members of the group who are experiencing difficulties are managed and mentored effectively.

Mentoring is becoming a popular way for groups to develop their staff. It also allows middle managers a forum to show that they are indeed blossoming leaders and can excel. Establishing and running a mentoring program is one of the best ways to help new members of the practice become a successful part of the group. It helps maintain the culture of the group and provides some guidance and expectations for performance and behavior. In addition, training and developing the group's staff will provide ample return on investment through increased skills, higher morale, and job satisfaction – all of which lead to happier patients.

Development and Training

One area of the organization that is often neglected is staff training and development. Larger medical groups might have a human resources department for this task, but smaller medical groups often do not have an organized function or department, so it falls to the medical practice executive to lead this effort.

Peter Senge[14] discusses extensively how the successful and competitive organization is one that is a "learning" organization, or one that learns as it goes about its daily activities. Learning is a deep-seated organizational value in these entities. In his book *Good to Great*,[15] James Collins talks about having the right people on the bus. In his thesis, being able to adapt is critical to being competitive. Learning is essential to adaptation, especially within the highly complex and technical environment of health care. It takes a high-functioning and ever-developing workforce to make an excellent team. Teaming largely is a function of staff development and it is the responsibility of the governing body to have these important functions clearly addressed. Every member of the group, employee or physician, should have:

- Development goals;

- Continuing professional education, either in-house or at away meetings; and

- Professional career goals that relate to organizational goals.

Every performance appraisal should include these goals, because what is rewarded and valued is what is usually received in the organization.

Adults learn in different styles and ways. Some prefer to go to a class, surrounded by others in similar situations, and discuss ideas and tasks in a group. Others prefer reading a "how to" book, attending an online program, or listening to an audiotape. Still others feel that they cannot learn unless they perform the task at hand. Understanding which learning style is most effective for each staff member results in a higher retention rate.

Rewards

By their very nature, people respond to rewards. Motivational rewards, such as a day off, a staff outing, or a celebration of successes, whether for the team and for individuals, enhance the group practice morale. Not every reward must be centered on monetary bonuses, which tend to dominate many medical practices' ideals for rewarding good behavior. For example, promotions or title changes can be extremely motivational. In addition, removing a distasteful task from someone's job description for a job well done is a reward in itself. A note or letter of recognition and achievement, recognizing and announcing "star" behavior at staff meetings, or buying the staff lunchroom a new microwave or comfortable chairs for relaxing are all ways to show appreciation.

■ Human Dynamics

Health care institutions, like many organizations, often focus on competencies, talents, and skills rather than personality traits in determining the success of individuals in the job. All are necessary for a successful human resource perspective; however, personality has a significant influence on the governance and the organizational dynamics of the medical group. Today, this aspect of human dynamics is beginning to receive a great deal of attention. A number of systems are currently being used to help evaluate personality and determine organizational fit. Two of these systems are the DISC system and the Predictive Index®, or PI.

DISC System

The DISC system[16] is based on the work of William M. Marston.[17] His work formed the foundation for a system of personality typing for

- Dominance;
- Inducement;

- Steadiness; and
- Compliance.

The system has predictive value in determining how an individual is likely to behave in a stressful situation. A personality type can be determined by testing individuals. The following nine associated behavioral styles of that personality type can be considered in this analysis:

1. Aggressive-Analytical;
2. Aggressive-Persuasive;
3. Persuasive-Forceful;
4. Persuasive-Diplomatic;
5. Persistent-Determined;
6. Conservative-Personable;
7. Cautious-Restrained;
8. Aggressive-Perfectionist; or
9. Persuasive-Persistent.

The Predictive Index

The PI,[18] like the DISC system, seeks to type an individual's personality by using four basic factors:

1. Factor A, or dominance;
2. Factor B, or introvert or extrovert;
3. Factor C, or patience; or
4. Factor D, or formal behavior.

The PI also includes two additional factors: M, or energy level, and E, or subjectivity and objectivity. Through a testing process, which will not be reviewed here, personality type can be determined, and an associated behavioral profile can then be created.

Understanding the personality types of a group and its members increases the opportunity to significantly improve the interaction of group members with one another and with the staff. This understanding provides a common language to discuss how individuals handle and express themselves differently in low-stress, or favorable, situations as well as in high-stress, or unfavorable, situations.

Understanding the behavioral characteristics of the group's membership will help to determine how best to motivate change. Change and improvement in the group has to move all members forward so that median behavior (M), median productivity (P), and any characteristic (C) has the effect of shifting the entire group's performance (see Exhibit 9).

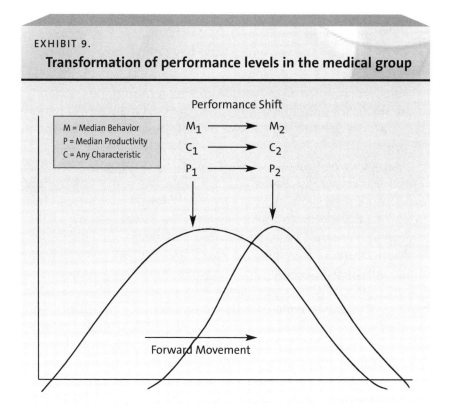

EXHIBIT 9.

Transformation of performance levels in the medical group

Performance Shift

M = Median Behavior
P = Median Productivity
C = Any Characteristic

$M_1 \longrightarrow M_2$

$C_1 \longrightarrow C_2$

$P_1 \longrightarrow P_2$

Forward Movement

■ Empowered Organizations

The governance structure of most medical groups is best character-ized as professional and collegial. Although a central operating committee or board may be vested with specific authorities as out-lined under the group's bylaws, a wise governance system provides ample opportunity for significant, meaningful collaboration with all members of the organization in the decision-making process. Governance structure must create the environment for constructive organizational dynamics. As legendary Notre Dame football coach Lou Holtz once said, "I have three operating principles of life, and they work for football as well:

1. Do your best.

2. Do what is right.

3. Treat others the way you would have others treat you."

This also works for a medical group practice. Holtz describes the values of an empowered organization, which need to be the nature of the medical group practice because the governance structure of the group significantly influences the culture and the operations of the organization.

Many groups function as confederations of people, with little central leadership. Decisions are made by consensus, which often leads to poor decision making or no decision at all. The modern group practice needs to move beyond this model. Strong, skilled leadership will result in better decision making.

More centralized systems of governance do not need to stifle input, but they must prevent the group from being stifled by a minority dissent that could delay or completely derail decision making. The phenomena of very small dissenting groups prevent-ing change or decision making are very divisive and present a diffi-cult way to run a substantial organization. It is detrimental to the group because any individual who has a differing opinion about a topic, and sometimes completely vested in his or her own self-interest, can have a significant impact on the outcome of that deci-sion through a filibustering or lobbying process.

Governance by consensus is frequently nonproductive and is totally antithetical to an effective operation. The board or governance body of the group exists only when it is in session. While in session, the board should act only to further the organization's mission.

Accountability for decisions in an opportunistic organization, such as a medical group, can be very problematic. In an article titled "7 Habits of Spectacularly Unsuccessful Executives,"[19] Sydney Finkelstein writes from the perspective of a large stock company, but his "habits" offer a number of apparent lessons for the medical group:

1. *Seeing themselves and their companies as dominating the environment – or the myth of preeminence.* Many medical groups feel they are the best because of credentials or reputation; however, this perspective can change very quickly as new competitors innovate and supply the market with better service and a more caring delivery of the increasingly fungible "high-quality care."

2. *Mixing business with pleasure.* Group members identify so completely with the group that there is no clear boundary between their personal interests and their business interests. Although there certainly is much room for pride and ownership views in the medical group, physicians see themselves as the reason for the success of the group and do not see the efforts of the whole group as a team.

3. *"Knowing" all the answers.* As skilled as medicine is, there are usually proscribed ways of approaching diagnosis and decision making that are clearly and carefully learned in training from the earliest days of medical school. Unfortunately, many groups do not use good processes to make critical decisions about the business, and rely too often on the quick judgment of the governing body. The environment of the medical group is faced with government issues, multiple payers, market forces, multiple stakeholders, changing technology, a changing workforce, and many other elements – all

with their own dynamics, making uncertainty the norm and not the rule.

4. *Ruthlessly eliminating anyone who isn't 100 percent behind them.* Most medical groups are not good at incorporating dissent into the process of decision making and assessment. They tend to take dissent as a personal attack and reject it.

5. *Obsession with image.* Not wanting to discuss problems is normal, but that doesn't mean an issue should not be resolved. Group members often make too many excuses for colleagues who misbehave, or overlook a trait or behavior in a colleague that they would not tolerate in a competitor or in themselves.

6. *Underestimating obstacles.* The medical group is often in a position of not knowing what resources will be needed to accomplish a particular goal. Because the task is not fully understood, the group may underestimate the time and other resources needed to complete the task and then become impatient with its progress.

7. *Stubbornly relying on what worked in the past.* Another way to put this is resistance to change. Medical groups often see individual efforts as the key to success. That may have been true in the past, but today, group efforts and the team approach will more likely lead to success. The business model in health care is changing rapidly.

Facilitate Physician Understanding and Acceptance of Good Business Management

■ Best Practices

A significant body of research exists on medical group practices and the traits that distinguish better-performing organizations. According to data published by MGMA,[20] better-performing groups have the following characteristics:

- A productivity-oriented culture in the group, and usually rewarded by physician compensation;
- Excellent communication between physicians and administrative staff;
- An emphasis on quality care, reputation, and patient satisfaction;
- A physician administrative leadership team in place;
- A good relationship with referral physicians;
- Excellent control systems and budgets;
- Known and understood cost structures;

- Central organization (delegation of decision making as opposed to consensus);
- A staff focus on customer service;
- Consideration of fit within the group and its culture in recruitment of new physicians;
- Delegation of management to administration;
- Administration seen as professional colleagues and specialists in business; and
- A culture of respect.

Teaching Best Practices

Physicians did not go to medical school to learn how to run a business. So, getting a physician to embrace good business practices with these characteristics is a task that takes time. The medical practice executive must become the teacher and provide continuous opportunities for physicians to understand and learn how good businesses operate and what they look like. Good leaders are good educators, and physicians are excellent students.

One way to teach physicians about business is to present examples of their own practice's business. For example, at a "lunch-and-learn" session, the medical practice executive can teach physicians about the following:

- The business "overview";
- Benchmarking;
- Service excellence;
- The health care markets;
- Overhead;
- Coding (understanding how to categorize);
- Compliance (necessary for survival); and
- How to read a financial statement.

The medical practice executive can supply a primer and coach physicians through the process. Shadowing is also a good strategy for such teaching topics as coding and compliance. To do this, certain staff members can spend time working with the physician during the daily routine. Every significant business meeting should be seen as an opportunity to teach, so every agenda should contain a topic related to understanding the business.

It is critical to the group's success that everyone "owns" the business – with its problems and opportunities alike. The practice cannot be seen as the administrator's overhead, the collection manager's collection rate, and the physician's profit. This attitude simply doesn't work in a fast-moving and often difficult environment. It also leads to dysfunctional business behavior because administrators become fearful of disclosing information that physicians may be unable to process and understand, but training the physicians can easily solve this problem.

Physicians must understand that they affect every aspect of the profit equation:

$$\text{Profit} = \text{Revenue} - \text{Expenses}$$

The medical practice executive should explain the components of this equation – in particular, where they come from and how they interact.

Patience is essential because it often takes years, as do many academic endeavors, to learn the business end of the practice. It is also essential that the medical practice executive be proactive in communications about the business. The effective administrator does not wait until the questions are asked, but seeks opportunities to answer questions before they are asked by looking at the various reporting documents through the eyes of the stakeholders. The medical practice executive will build credibility as well as trust if he or she creates a group training and education plan and executes it.

Quality of Patient Care

The availability of health care information has greatly increased in recent years. The Internet has led to a revolution in the information available to patients about health care services, facilities, and providers. In effect, the Internet is democratizing health care. A recent search on Google found 1,673,334 Websites related to health care.

Data are being collected by many organizations, both commercial and nonprofit. Programs such as "Bridges to Excellence" provide patients with:

- Research on the quality of a physician or practice;
- Help to identify qualified physicians, based on the patient's criteria;
- An opportunity to express satisfaction or dissatisfaction regarding a physician encounter; and
- A way to find out what other patients have said about the physician.

Educated patients are informed consumers and may ask more questions of the physician and his/her treatment plan. Physicians can take this opportunity to have patients collaborate on their treatment, possibly making patients more compliant and satisfied.

■ Issues for Examination and Correction

Identifying the Issues

Among the many opportunities to evaluate the practice, some of the most fruitful for quality improvement activities are:

- Patient satisfaction surveys;
- Malpractice claims review;
- Benchmarking of clinical and nonclinical data;
- Standards established by specialty societies, such as the American College of Cardiology and the American College of Family Practice; and
- Review and understanding of national data, such as from the departments of the National Institutes of Health[21] and the Agency for Healthcare Research and Quality.[22]

Evaluating Issues

Initiatives on quality require a systematic approach to reduce the influence of bias and emotions on the process. Among the many techniques that have been used are:

- Total Quality Management (TQM);
- Continuous Quality Improvement (CQI); and
- Six Sigma.[23]

These techniques use statistical measures to evaluate an identified process to determine the source of error and variation in outcome. The many resources on each technique, easily found through a Web or library search, will offer more complete information.

As stated earlier in this task, one way to collect data on a group's patient population is to conduct patient satisfaction surveys. This single tool can provide significant insight into a practice's issues and challenges – as well as its stellar performance areas. The governing body should monitor and collect such data on the practice to understand what is happening within the group. See this volume's Task 3 for more information on surveys.

■ Organizational Goals

In healthy organizations, the staff's personal, professional, and organizational visions and values should align and focus on the organizational mission (see Exhibit 10). Otherwise, there is the risk of serious burnout. The board has to articulate organizational values and facilitate an understanding of what is expected and valued by the group. An example might be a culture of respect or patient service. This culture of respect has to be valued not by simply saying "we want it" or pretending that the culture exists when it doesn't, but by building it through behavior and action and by providing a consequence for inaction.

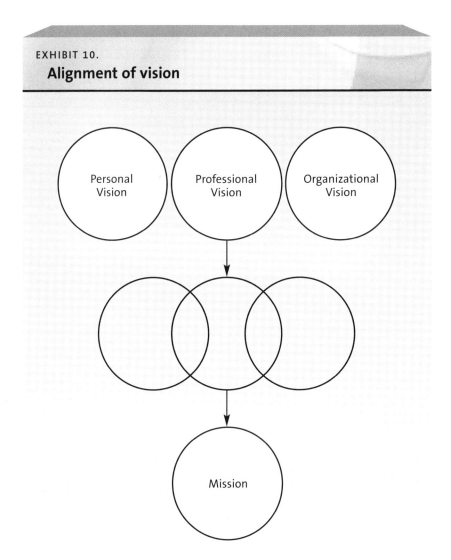

EXHIBIT 10.

Alignment of vision

■ Behavioral Characteristics of Clinical Staff

Shortages of physicians and staff are becoming commonplace in the health care organization. Negative behavior is often at the root of dissatisfaction, which leads to turnover and poor performance.

Medical groups, and the health care industry in general, have focused so much on technical competence that they have often ignored the personality traits that create a positive working environment.

Training, licensing, and proper technical competence are absolute requirements. Behavioral interviewing, however, is becoming more fashionable and will help match physician candidates and other employees with the desired behaviors that the group deems appropriate.

Behavioral interviewing begins with a consideration of desirable characteristics, such as those listed in Exhibit 11. These characteristics can then be used to develop interview questions and scenarios for the interview process.

EXHIBIT 11.

Definitions of desirable behavioral characteristics

Characteristic	Definition
Acceptance	Accepting of others; showing a strong tendency to notice and include those who feel left out
Achievement	Demonstrating great stamina, a positive work ethic, and a strong concern for production
Adaptability	Ability to "go with the flow," taking things as they come and discovering the future one day at a time
Agreeability	Demonstrating a desire to achieve consensus or agreement; conflict avoidant
Command	Presence; ability to take control of a situation and make decisions
Communication	Ability to put thoughts into words; good at conversation and presentation
Competitive	Demonstrating a strong desire to measure progress against standards and others; a desire to win
Confidence	Self-assurance; ability to manage one's life and make decisions with conviction

EXHIBIT 11. *(continued)*

Definitions of desirable behavioral characteristics

Characteristic	Definition
Cooperation	Accommodating the needs and interests of others; deferring one's own goals to assist others
Creativity	Finding practical applications and connections between seemingly disparate phenomena
Curiosity	Demonstrating a strong desire to collect, learn, and archive all kinds of information
Delegation	Ability to successfully enlist and capitalize on the talents of others to meet objectives
Deliberation	Taking serious care to ensure effective decisions and anticipate obstacles
Development	Tendency to cultivate improvements in others
Directness	Letting others know where they stand by using a straightforward and clear manner
Discipline	Demonstrating a strong desire for order, structure, and routine
Empathy	Sensing the feelings of others by imagining themselves in others' lives and situations
Energy	Making things happen by turning thoughts into action; often coupled with impatience, though
Enthusiasm	Tendency to be upbeat; ability to excite others about what needs to be done
Fairness	Demonstrating a strong need to treat all people the same, with clear rules and uniform enforcement
Focus	Taking direction, prioritizing, and following through and making necessary corrections to stay on track
Helpfulness	Demonstrating a strong desire to take actions to assist others
Improvement	Demonstrating a great desire to learn and continuously improve; process orientation
Independence	Preference for autonomy and ability to act with little or no direction
Influence	Ability to meet and win over others quickly

EXHIBIT 11. *(continued)*
Definitions of desirable behavioral characteristics

Characteristic	Definition
Innovative	Ability to comfortably handle fast-changing environments; willingness to try untested approaches
Intimacy	Demonstrating a strong desire for close relationships with others
Loyalty	Demonstrating a strong commitment to the organization; respecting and supporting those in authority
Organization	Figuring out how all pieces and resources can be arranged for maximum productivity
Personalization	Demonstrating a strong desire to understand the unique qualities of each person
Politeness	Demonstrating courtesy, manners, and rapport in personal interactions
Responsibility	Taking psychological ownership of what one says he or she will do
Resilience	Recovering quickly from stressful situations; remaining cool under pressure
Sociability	Seeking out and enjoying social interactions and social events
Strategic	Taking a long-range, broad approach to problem solving and decision making
Tactical	Focusing on short-range, hands-on, practical strategies to achieve immediate results

■ Patient Safety

Quality care and the rate of medical errors are becoming issues of great concern in the health care industry. A major barrier to change and improvement activities in medical groups is the problem of variation. Variation equals cost. This variation, as noted earlier, is one inherent reason for the slow growth of larger medical practices because of their inability to standardize processes. In addition, the variability in the delivery of care has been associated with quality issues such as fragmentation and the inability to leverage economies of scale in the physician practice to any significant degree.

In his book *Medical Nemesis*,[24] Ivan Illich delivers a stinging indictment of the health care system:

> The major threat to health in the world is modern medicine. The medical community has actually become a great threat to people. Doctors and others [pharmaceutical industry] serve their own interests first. People become consumers and objects.

Illich identifies three levels of damage:

1. Clinical treatment actually often harms people. Patient safety has not been a high priority.

2. More and more problems are being seen as appropriate for medical intervention, and pharmaceutical companies are developing expensive treatments for nondiseases.

3. More than 100,000 people die each year in the United States from adverse drug effects.

Develop and Implement Quality Assurance Programs

■ Quality Improvement and the Effective Medical Group

Quality of service provided by group practices is paramount to group practice operations and the future of health care, and, because of increased criticism of health care services, pay for performance is becoming a reality. Quality of service starts with an understanding of what the medical group is really about.

The first task of this volume discussed the many structures of medical practices and listed their attributes; however, in the past, organizing for delivery of quality was not a central theme for the medical group. Many structural and operational considerations took precedence over quality of care because quality was taken for granted. The lack of standardization, the absence of any formal adherence to best practices, and the lack of formalized quality improvement for programs all contribute to a lack of progress in this area.

Medical group structures are not designed, or in some cases are antithetically designed, to invest in quality initiatives. The ultra-short-term focus of financial performance is a chief culprit. Groups do not invest enough, either financially or in the training needed to carry out large-scale improvement initiatives. Investment dollars come only from the shareholders' pockets, a prospect that has long curtailed the development of modern medical groups.

In his book *Out of the Crisis*,[25] W. Edwards Deming asks a question that should serve as the cornerstone of any group's quality initiative:

What are you doing about the quality that you hope to provide to your customers four years from now?

The issue of quality in the U.S. health care system is becoming increasingly important as the issue of quality gains more understanding. For most of history, quality has been virtually undefined. As Plato would have said, it is indeed in the eye of the beholder. However, that is changing dramatically and will continue to do so as measures and expectations of quality of health care services continue to evolve.

■ Team Building

The process of team building is hardly a mystery. Effective team building is an essential responsibility of management and the governance structure of the medical group. Team building and a team-building culture must be developed because it is antithetical to the physician mentality – physicians are trained to work as individuals and to take personal accountability for their actions.

Interactions

Members of a group's governing body must be aware of their own personality and style and how they interact with one another. This is best achieved through personality testing and self-awareness training. The better the team understands its members' individual personalities and leadership styles, and, in general, how they interact with others, the better the team will be at organizational dynamics. For example, dominant personalities become very active when under pressure, which explains why meetings with a number of dominant personalities can often end with argument, conflict, and ultimate indecision. The same skills that may make for a great physician may be useless in the boardroom. Board and general group retreats are excellent ways to improve group dynamics.

Education

Annual retreats can provide educational opportunities, with a choice of topics, such as governance, leadership, business planning, benchmarking, best practices, group dynamics, policy, and legal issues, to focus on each year. In addition, courses, symposia, and other outside sources provide educational opportunities if physicians are given support to attend, meaning time as well as money. The group must encourage and value the development of leaders and demonstrate this by providing resources for the purpose.

In addition, the medical practice executive or other leader can provide an educational presentation at each group meeting, with all levels of staff. Presentations done in PowerPoint® can then be distributed to the group so any of the members can review the material or see it if they were unable to be at the presentation. An opportunity to discuss the material with group members is also a good idea. Examples of issues for such presentations are the Health Insurance Portability and Accountability Act of 1996 (HIPAA), Medicare and managed care contracts, and MGMA data.

Other successful educational activities include:

- A lending library of books and periodicals available to the group members;
- Several copies of a relevant book distributed to the group; and
- Regular e-mails of pertinent articles sent to the group.

Feedback

Processes that are logical and allow participation and input, such as nominal group techniques, surveys, interviews, and planned feedback, can determine if the practice's team-building activities are welcome and have the desired outcome.

Empowering Teams

As mentioned earlier, one of the greatest deficiencies in group practice administration is physicians' lack of business training and education. This includes the physicians-at-large in the group, as well as those in the governing body. Physician leaders must be groomed, trained, mentored, and educated in the key elements of business success for the medical practice, including working as a team. As with any good orientation program, the assumption is that no one knows anything about governance or how they should behave or function as board members.

The fundamentals of empowering a team are to value team members and their input and to thank the team members regularly, not just when they "leap over tall buildings." Recognition of the team, financially and otherwise, is an important part of team empowerment. Assessment of the team should be part of the performance appraisal process. Celebrate successes as a team in some fun activity. Celebrations can be as simple as a pizza party or they can involve community activities, such as working on a Habitat for Humanity house, volunteering with United Way, participating in an American Heart Association Heart Walk, or helping in a hospital fundraiser.

■ Industry Quality Benchmarks

Medical group practice quality initiatives should be led and passionately promoted by the governance structures of the group. A pay-for-performance program, accreditation, malpractice, and consumer demand all work to create an increasing expectation of continually improving patient care that can be demonstrated by objective data and systematic measurement. The National Committee on Quality Assurance (NCQA) has led this effort for more than two decades. Activities include many quality initiatives focused on practice profiles, practice guidelines based on evidence-based data, education of practitioners, and health plans for patients. The Health Plan Employer Data and Information Set (HEDIS) report evaluates health plans through measurement of their specific performance in a number of quality areas, such as prevention, screening of patients, and other clinical measures.

Practices may seek accreditation by providing data about their activities including clinical measures required by NCQA that are submitted during the accreditation process.[26]

Satisfaction Surveys

Satisfaction surveys are essential to evaluating an organization and are a cornerstone of quality improvement programs. For satisfaction surveys to be successful, a number of factors are important. Surveying is a widely studied area. A great deal of information is available to help guide the surveying strategy of the group.

- *The testing should be simple and reproducible.* This is an activity that may be worth outsourcing to a testing company that can provide survey tools and analysis.

- *Concerns that are identified in the survey should be addressed.* Surveys should not ask about things that the practice is not prepared to address because that will only create additional dissatisfaction. This may also be true for issues that the practice may not have control over, such as patients' health plans. Patient satisfaction does correlate to health plans, but the practice has little opportunity to address those issues.

- *The questions should be simple, direct, and short.* This is especially true of general surveys. Focus groups or more in-depth surveys may be appropriate when addressing specific issues (e.g., the need for evening and weekend hours).

- *The validity of the questions should be examined through statistical analysis.* In other words, question outcomes should actually correlate with satisfaction.

- *The practice should design specific interventions for problem areas* and use these plans as opportunities to educate the staff and physicians.

- *Surveys should be repeated on a regular schedule and the results tracked over time.* This will help to evaluate intervention success. Satisfaction is a matter for the entire group, not just the administration, governing board, or the physicians, so this information should be shared with everyone in the organization.

■ Benchmarking

Although performance measurements are covered very well in other volumes in the *Medical Practice Management Body of Knowledge Review Series*, benchmarking, preparation of dashboards, and report cards are some of the best ways for the governing body of the group to monitor organizational goals. Benchmarks produce a quick, easy-to-understand, and high-impact way to communicate essential information.

It is important to develop a series of benchmarks that can be tracked over time to monitor the progress and status of the group performance. This will include quality indicators, such as results of quality initiatives, comparisons with peer databases, and financial indicators such as:

- Gross Revenue/per RVU;
- Collections/per RVU;
- Profit/Net Income/per RVU;
- RVU per MD;
- Operating Cost/per RVU; and
- Employee Salary/per RVU.

Relative Value Units (RVUs) make excellent measurement tools because they have become a standard part of group practice management and reimbursement systems. They have universal applicability and recognition.[27]

Exhibit 12 is an example of a simple benchmarking report card that can be used by a governing body to monitor organizational performance.

Benchmarks need to be understandable. They must communicate their meaning clearly, be reproducible over time, and be current for quickly reacting to changing situations. Benchmarks also need to measure key competencies or key success indicators for the practice.

In summary, benchmarking allows the governing body to:

- Compare the practice to those of successful peers;[28]

- Communicate in times of rapid change when internal signposts are less clear;

EXHIBIT 12.
Sample quarterly report – 3-year comparison

	1st Qtr 2004 Conversion Factor: 36.3167 Total RVUs = 303, 264		1st Qtr 2005 Conversion Factor: 38.2581 Total RVUs = 324,016		1st Qtr 2006 Conversion Factor: 36.1992 Total RVUs = 316,326	
	Totals	$ Per RVU	Totals	$ Per RVU	Totals	$ Per RVU
Gross Revenue	$12,821,311	$42	$14,918,834	$46	$14,648,065	$46
Collections	12,814,986	42	14,773,024	46	14,405,557	46
Profit/ Net Income	1,765,542	6	2,774,379	9	1,804,222	6
Operating Cost	6,793,882	22	7,602,643	23	8,391,248	27
Employee Salary	2,740,441	9	3,125,846	10	14,918,834	47

Physician Productivity Measures per Quarter

Total RVUs	303,264		324,016		316,326	
	No. of MDs	RVUs per MD	No of MDs	RVUs per MD	No. of MDs	RVUs per MD
	50	6,065	55	5,856	58	5,471

- Analyze activity (by using internal and external benchmarks);
- Evaluate specific procedures and processes (e.g., collection, profitability);
- Take action on a specific need or problem; and
- Evaluate change.

Benchmark Characteristics

The key characteristics of benchmarks are that they should be:

- Relevant to the business and measure key indicators that drive profitability, quality, or other critical success factors;
- Timely – old news is no news;
- Able to differentiate between accountable items (e.g., whether each benchmark provides new information);
- Adaptable and adoptable, so physicians and staff can learn from peers; and
- Consistent, using the same metrics each time (e.g., not using RVUs during one period of time, only to change to a dollars-per-unit of service on the next).

Benchmarking Problems

It may be difficult to evaluate the effects of individual variations in processes, variables, and other parameters. It is therefore important that the practice should not expect too much from the benchmarking process; it is not a substitute for good management, it is only a tool.

Surprisingly little profit variation may be explained by the usual causes. This can lead to classic strategic errors in correcting a perceived problem. Therefore, a number of indicators should be considered, and over time those that correlate best with the business will become apparent.

Every governing body faces the challenge of effectively monitoring data about the well-being of the practice without trying to glean this information from raw data or detailed reports.

Dashboards and benchmarking report cards are useful for this purpose and can be prepared by the finance department or administration. A detailed review of data should be reserved for areas of concern. By benchmarking key financial and other important practice parameters, the board can effectively monitor the critical activities of practice performance and fulfill this important obligation to the members of the group.

■ Dashboards

A practice dashboard is a technique that uses simple visual indications of how a particular activity is progressing in absolute terms or in terms relative to a goal. As can be seen in Exhibit 13, this simple

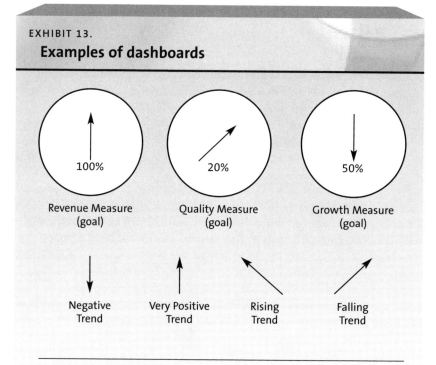

EXHIBIT 13.
Examples of dashboards

100%
Revenue Measure (goal)

20%
Quality Measure (goal)

50%
Growth Measure (goal)

Negative Trend

Very Positive Trend

Rising Trend

Falling Trend

Simple representation of positive and negative trends can often be useful to quickly communicate a great deal of information effectively.

representation of positive and negative trends can quickly communicate a great deal of information effectively. This feature is especially useful when meeting time is limited because information presented in this manner reduces the need to interpret detailed reports.

Most medical groups prepare profit-and-loss (P&L) statements on a regular basis. Such financial records and documents are essential and helpful for the medical practice executive, but many do little to guide strategic issues or to plan for the future. Two essential financial planning instruments are the budget and the pro forma financial statement.

The budget provides a financial look into the future based upon proposed activities of the group. The budget steps that the medical plan executive follows in preparing the budget for the group are as follows:

Step 1: Perform an environmental assessment and strategic plan review.

Step 2: Establish the budget guidelines.

Step 3: Provide detailed forecasts, and historical and comparative information.

Step 4: Review forecast against the guidelines.

Step 5: Revise as necessary.

Step 6: Submit to board for presentation and approval.

The pro forma financial statement is essentially an estimate of the profit and loss from a particular service or proposed activity. It would involve all of the steps that are necessary for preparing a P&L statement, but in most cases, much of the information is estimated based upon what is expected.

Modeling

Although budgets and pro formas essentially are financial models of the medical group as a whole (budget) or of a particular service (pro forma), more specific modeling data can be developed to guide practice planning and development. The medical practice executive should understand the concepts of variable costs, fixed costs, and revenue data. For example, if one were to consider opening a satellite office in a new city, many strategic reasons may be important and would contribute to making the decision to open this office, but certainly financial considerations and modeling would be important. If patients and revenue growth are the goals of opening the new office, then a model that allows the enterprise to calculate the number of patients required to generate particular revenue would be important.

Such data can be modeled based on reasonable assumptions, which can be gained from the typical practice management system. For example:

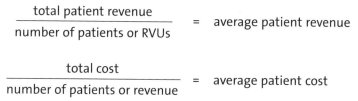

$$\frac{\text{total patient revenue}}{\text{number of patients or RVUs}} = \text{average patient revenue}$$

$$\frac{\text{total cost}}{\text{number of patients or revenue}} = \text{average patient cost}$$

Assumptions about variables such as age, diagnosis, and time can all be included to help create a forecasting model of a new location or service. Typically, expenses are much easier to forecast than revenue for any practice activity because expenses are more easily identifiable. Other valuable data include the frequency of the service on a national or regional basis and the frequency of the diagnosis on a national or regional basis. Much of these data are available from MGMA.

As electronic patient records and better practice management systems are developed, modeling will become easier, faster, more accurate, and therefore, more useful.

Conclusion

LIKE A LIVING ORGANISM, the medical group must understand itself and its environment and respond appropri-
ately and in a focused way. The governance process can
no longer be the static "caretaker" function of the past,
but must be tantamount to a new leadership mechanism
for the group – the medical practice executive. The governing body must unify, provide vision, and inspire those
being governed. Furthermore, it has to communicate the
mission of the organization in a clear and effective way.

The governance and organizational dynamics of the
medical group require careful attention. The tasks
described and discussed in this volume are essential to
maintaining a functional group and are equally important to creating an environment where change is possible.
Change is a fundamental ingredient to becoming the
place of choice for patients, physicians, and employees.
This process starts with good governance and attention to
organizational dynamics and continues by developing a
mastery of the related skills and tools. These tools are a
balance of art and science. Proper governance depends on
a keen insight into all of the members of the organization: Who they are? What motivates them? How do they
relate to one another? What values do they share?

Modern medical group practice administration and,
to a large degree, medical group governance are about the
management of relationships with all of the various stakeholders and constituent groups. These stakeholders

include physicians, patients, employees, hospitals, community leaders, payers, and many more. Without a clear structure for governance, and managing these relationships, the organization simply will not produce the level of performance expected.

Exercises

THESE QUESTIONS have been retired from the ACMPE Essay Exam question bank. Because there are so many ways to handle various situations, there are no "right" answers, and thus, no answer key. Use these questions to help you practice responses in different scenarios.

1. You are a new administrator of a medical practice. An older partner has recently relinquished management responsibilities to another partner. During your first six months, the former managing partner continues to question and override the new managing partner's decisions and is adamant that you follow his instructions.

   Describe how you would handle this situation.

2. You are the administrator for a primary care medical practice serving a growing suburban community. It is becoming increasingly difficult to schedule patient appointments, and waiting times are increasing. The physicians disagree about the need to recruit new providers.

    Describe how you would handle this situation.

3. You are the administrator of a four-physician family practice group that is merging with a three-physician family practice group. Your most senior physician has expressed concern over the younger physicians in the other group working shorter hours and taking more vacation time. Although both practices would benefit from the economies of scale of a merger, the senior physician is concerned about the disparate philosophies of the two practices. The managing partner of your practice disagrees and strongly favors proceeding.

Describe how you would handle this situation.

4. You are the administrator of a medical practice. The physicians have been arguing about how they should divide up expenses. The higher-producing physicians want all expenses to continue to be divided equally, and the low producers are demanding that costs be split based on gross production. Expense distribution has been an issue for years, but in recent months the debate has become contentious.

    Discuss how you would help the physicians resolve this issue.

5. You are the administrator of a medical practice that has grown from 10 to 25 physicians over a five-year period. It is getting more difficult to get all board members together, and you have been unable to obtain a quorum at the most recently scheduled meeting.

Describe how you would handle this situation.

6. You are the administrator of a cardiology practice. Eighteen
    months ago, three of your younger physicians left to set up
    a competing group across town. Of your remaining five
    physicians, two are contemplating retirement in the next
    two years. Your staff has repeatedly expressed concern to
    you regarding the future of the practice, and in the past
    month, you have lost several key nursing and business
    office personnel. In addition, some of your staff have heard
    the physicians openly talking about not meeting payroll,
    and they are profoundly upset.

    Describe how you would handle this situation.

7. You are the administrator of a single-specialty group. Your group has become divided due to differing opinions about the group's income distribution methodology. The administrative stipend allocated for the chair of the board is now being criticized in light of the group's declining net income. However, the increase in managed care contracting requires the board chair to spend more time on administrative responsibilities. The board chair feels that the administrative stipend should be increased because she has less time to devote to patient care and is spending increased efforts on the group's behalf. The criticism has elevated to the point that even the staff is becoming visibly anxious. You are concerned that if the situation is not resolved, the group may dissolve, or at the least, the group's reputation will be harmed as the discontent becomes more publicly known.

   Describe how you would address this problem.

8. You are the administrator of a six-physician general surgery practice. For some time now, your doctors have been aware of the decreasing profitability of the practice. They are beginning to explore ways to increase revenue and/or decrease expenses. You have reviewed the group's financial information and feel that expenses have already been reduced as much as possible. The last quarter has shown a consistent negative bottom line. Your analysis shows that the most viable options are for the physicians to increase productivity or reduce their personal income. You have been asked to prepare a recommendation for next week's board meeting.

    Describe how you would address this situation.

Notes

1. Robert's Rules of Order can be found on the Internet at www.constitution.org/rror/rror--00.htm.

2. Institute of Medicine, *To Err Is Human: Building a Safer Health System* (Washington, D.C.: Institute of Medicine, 1999).

3. Stephen L. Wagner, "Defining the ACMPE Fellow," *College View* (Fall 2003): 27–30.

4. Henry Mintzberg, "Five Ps for Strategy" in *The Strategy Process*, H. Mintzberg and J. B. Quinn, Eds. (Englewood Cliffs, N.J.: Prentice-Hall International Editions, 1992): 12–19.

5. Michael E. Porter, *Competitive Strategy: Techniques for Analyzing Industries and Competitors* (New York: The Free Press, 1980): 47–74.

6. Ibid., 35.

7. Patrick Lencioni, *The Five Dysfunctions of a Team: A Leadership Fable* (San Francisco: Jossey-Bass, 2002): 195–221.

8. Ralph Stayer, "How I Learned to Let My Workers Lead," *Harvard Business Review* (November/December 1990): 66–88.

9. *Robert's Rules of Order Revised,* www.constitution.org/rror/rror--00.htm

10. Don A. Dillman, *Mail and Telephone Surveys: The Total Design Method* (New York: John Wiley & Sons, Inc., 1978): 79–149.

11. D. R. Berdie, J. F. Anderson, & M. A. Niebuhr, *Questionnaires: Design and Use* (Metuchen, N.J. & London: The Scarecrow Press, 1986).

12. R. T. Hurlburt, *Comprehending Behavioral Statistics*, 3rd ed. (Belmont, Calif.: Wadsworth/Thompson Learning, 2003).

13. SPSS.com, www.spss.com.

14. Peter Senge, *The Fifth Discipline* (New York: Currency, 1999): 233–272.

15. James Collins, *Good to Great: Why Some Companies Make the Leap... and Others Don't* (New York: HarperCollins, 2001).

16. L.F. McManus Company, Inc., 370 Main Street, Worcester, Mass. 01608-1714.

17. William, M. Marston, *The Emotions of Normal People* (New York: Harcourt-Brace and Company, 1928). This book in its entirety is the basis for the DISC system.

18. Praendex Incorporated, P.O. Box 888464, Atlanta, Ga.

19. Sydney Finkelstein, "7 Habits of Spectacularly Unsuccessful Executives," *Fast Company* (July 2003): 84–89.

20. Medical Group Management Association (MGMA), "Group Practice – Governance and Organizational Charts – Questionnaire Results, Information Exchange" (Englewood, Colo.: Medical Group Management Association, June 1999).

21. National Institutes of Health, www.nih.gov/icd (retrieved July 2005).

22. Agency for Healthcare Research and Quality, www.ahcpr.gov/.

23. "What Is Six Sigma?" www.sixsigmasystems.com/what_is_six_sigma.html.

24. Ivan Illich, *Medical Nemesis: The Exploration of Health* (New York: Random House, 1976).

25. W. Edwards Deming, *Out of the Crisis* (Cambridge, Mass.: Massachusetts Institute of Technology, Center for Advanced Engineering Studies, 1990): 166.

26. National Committee for Quality Assurance, www.ncqa.org/ (retrieved July 2005).

27. Kathryn Glass, *RVUs: Applications for Medical Practice Success* (Englewood, Colo.: Medical Group Management Association, 2003).

28. Medical Group Management Association (MGMA), *Performance and Practices of Successful Medical Groups* (Englewood, Colo.: Medical Group Management Association, 2004).

Glossary

Active leadership – A form of leadership that requires constant involvement of the leader and a keen awareness of the operational issues confronting the company.

Adaptiveness – Flexibility; the ability to respond to change.

Anchoring – A concept in decision making that correlates the influence of prior information received by the decision maker on his or her decision.

Attitudes – A mental state of readiness.

Behavior – Anything that a person does.

Commitment to mission – A complete focus on the mission of the organization that tends not to change quickly or without serious reevaluation. The amount of effort involved in the achievement of organizational goals.

Dashboard – Similar to a car's dashboard; the "driver" can use this technique to take a visionary view of the practice's internal markers and indicators, as well as the road ahead by asking: What's in the way? Is the road clear of obstacles and traffic? Also known as an operational dashboard, this activity provides medical practice and other business executives with a continuous, up-to-date analysis of key business information (not data) that is integrated and consistent, providing a continuous view of the group's current – and immediate future – situation.

Decision-making styles –

Analytical style – Decision maker gives careful consideration to unique situations and is a rational thinker; typical when there is a higher tolerance for ambiguity.

Behavioral style – Decision maker wants to avoid conflict or places greater importance on social relationships and is receptive to suggestions.

Conceptual style – Decision maker is an intuitive rather than rational thinker; seen when there is a high level of ambiguity.

Directive style – Decision maker tends to be a rational thinker; minimal information is used and few alternatives are given for considerations; typically adopted where and when tolerance for ambiguity is low.

Decision paralysis – The inability to make decisions in a timely manner due to problems with decision-making styles or methods.

Decision rules – Explicit and implicit statements, procedures, and ways of thinking (influenced by decision-making styles) that determine how decisions are made by individuals and organizations.

Dysfunctional conflict – An interaction or conflict between groups that harms the organization and hinders goal achievement.

Environmental factors – Forces that influence the business but are external to the business itself. Examples include public policy, regulations, and economic conditions.

Functional conflict – A confrontation between individuals or groups that improves organization goal achievement.

Goal – A specific target that an individual or company tries to achieve.

Governance – A system of policies and procedures designed to oversee the management of the enterprise. Governance is the foundation of how the practice will behave, compete, and document its actions.

Group culture – How the group conducts its business. Culture is a series of formal and informal processes, beliefs, values, and norms.

Informational disequilibrium – A situation characterized by one party to a exchange having significantly more information about the subject matter than the other party.

Micromanagement – Usually used to describe a situation in which a governing body inappropriately engages in the management activities of the company.

Mission – The purpose of the organization; what is expected of the organization by its stakeholders.

Operational activities – The processes that carry out the functional planning, policies, and procedures of the organization.

Operational knowledge – The body of information, which is necessary to effectively understand how the business works and what drives success.

Organization communication pathways – All of the formal and informal ways that communications occur in an organization, such as e-mail, memos, meetings, and verbal communications.

Organizational change – A process of evolving that helps the company adapt to a new set of environmental and competitive factors.

Organizational dynamics – The script for the organization's human capital; the ways in which individuals and processes interact within the company.

Parking lot – A meeting-management technique where items unrelated to the agenda are recorded separately for later attention.

Process improvement techniques – A number of processes are used to systematically examine and measure various aspects of the practice to determine ways to improve operations and outcomes.

Programmed decisions – Structured problems that involve goals that are clear and are often familiar because they have occurred before. Structured problems are easily and completely defined with complete and available information.

Shift of paradigms – A change in the way a company views its business and processes.

Stakeholders – All of the individuals and groups that have a vested interest in the activities of the organization.

Strategy – The science of business planning whereby an organization determines its focus and major initiatives for future activity.

SWOT – A strategic planning technique that systematically looks at a company's strengths, weaknesses, opportunities, and threats.

Transformational leadership – A series of actions by governing bodies and management that allow the company to evolve to changing needs caused by technological, environmental, and competitive changes in the industry.

Values – The beliefs and guidelines an individual uses to make choices when confronted with a situation.

Bibliography

Agency for Healthcare Research and Quality (AHRQ). www.ahrq.gov.

Bachrach, David. "How Does the Governing Body of Your Faculty Practice Plan Stack Up?" *MGMA e-Connexion*, no. 57 (July 2004).

Berglund, Ronald G. "The World Is Working to Improve Health Care." *Health Care Weekly Review*, Special Reprint 4 (April 2001).

Bohlmann, Robert C. "Physician Leadership: The Revolving-Door Debate." *MGMA Connexion* 4, no. 1 (2004): 15–16.

Bost, Brent W. "Take It to the Max: The Importance of Physician Ownership in Integrated Delivery Systems." *MGMA Connexion* 3, no. 4 (April 2003): 28–29.

Bradford, Vicky. "Making Your Case for Change: A Template to Follow." *MGMA Connexion* 3, no. 7 (2003): 28–29.

Brown, Packard. "Safeguard Board Value: Allow Alternative Viewpoints." *MGMA e-Connexion* (February 2004).

Burney, Robert. "The JCAHO Approach to Medical Errors." *American Society for Quality's 55th Annual Quality Conference Proceedings* (Milwaukee: ASQ, 2001), 743.

Carey, Raymond G., & Robert C. Lloyd. *Measuring Quality Improvement in Health Care: A Guide to Statistical Process Control Applications* (New York: Quality Resources, a Division of the Kraus Organization Limited, 1995).

Chaplin, Ed. "Comprehensive Quality Function Deployment: Beyond the Seven Basic Quality Tools." *American Society for Quality Health Care Division Newsletter* (Spring 2001): 5.

Chowdhury, S. *The Power of Six Sigma* (Chicago: Dearborn Trade, 2000), 29.

Edsel, William M. "By the Book: Lessons Learned from Developing a Physician-Owners' Manual." *MGMA Connexion* 4, no. 5 (2004): 40–43.

Fabrizio, Nick. "Achieving Organizational Flexibility to Cope with a Changing Healthcare Environment." ACMPE professional paper (Englewood, Colo.: American College of Medical Practice Executives, 2004).

Gabel, Stewart. "Making Waves: Stages and Process of Organizational Change." *MGMA Connexion* 3, no. 9 (2003): 31–32.

Galbraith, Jay. *Designing Organizations* (San Francisco: Jossey-Bass, 1995).

Gans, David. "Following a Road Map to Success." *MGMA Connexion* 3, no. 6 (2003): 26–27.

Gibson, James L., John M. Ivancevich, James H. Donnelly, & Robert Konopaske. *Organizations: Behavior, Structure, Processes*, 11th ed. (New York: McGraw-Hill/Irwin, 2002).

Hansen, Richard D. "Physician and Administrator Leadership: Why Different Is Good." *MGMA Connexion* 3, no. 2 (2003): 28.

Hertz, Kenneth T. "Meeting Management: Get the Most from Your Gatherings." *MGMA Connexion* 4, no. 5 (2004): 49–53.

Hyde, Margaret O. *Your Brain Master Computer* (New York: McGraw-Hill Book Company, 1964).

Institute for Manufacturing at Cambridge University, Cambridge, UK. www.ifm.eng.cam.ac.uk/dstools/ (retrieved 2005).

McManus, L. F. *Self Perception: A Profile Analysis* (Worcester, Mass.: L.F. McManus Company, Inc., 2001.)

Mertz, Gregory J. "Consider It Job Security: Creating an Effective Physician-Administrator Team." *MGMA Connexion* 3, no. 10 (2003): 30–31.

———. "Effective Physician Governance Is Not an Oxymoron." *MGMA Connexion* 3, no. 1 (2003): 50–53.

National Institutes of Health. "HHS Launches New Efforts to Promote Paperless Health Care System." (Baltimore: National Institutes of Health, National Library of Medicine, July 1, 2003).

National Institutes of Health, Office of Extramural Research. "Funding Opportunities and Notices." U.S. Department of Health and Human Services, "NIH Guide: Transforming Healthcare Quality through Information Technology (THQIT) – Planning Grants," Request for Applications (RFA) Number: RFA-HS-04-010 (also see NOT-HS-04-001, release date: November 20, 2003. Available via search page at http://grants.nih.gov/grants/guide/index.html. Document directly retrieved at http://grants.nih.gov/grants/guide/rfa-files/RFA-HS-04-010.html.

National Library of Medicine (NLM). www.nlm.nih.gov.

Orlikoff, James E., E. George Middleton Jr., Dennis R. Barry, Kathryn J. McDonagh, J. Larry Tyler, & Errol L. Biggs. "Old Board/New Board: Governance in an Era of Accountability." *Frontiers of Health Services Management* 21, no. 3 (Spring 2005).

Palatchi, Karen E. "Join the Crowd: Moving from Rugged Individualists to Collaborating Group Members." *MGMA Connexion* 3, no. 4 (2003): 42–47.

Pande, P., R. Neuman, & R. Cavanagh. *The Six Sigma Way – How GE, Motorola and Other Top Companies Are Honing Their Performance* (New York: McGraw-Hill, 2000), 23–24.

"Physicians Practice Compliance Report." *MGMA and Opus Publications* 3, no. 1 (January 2000).

Pope, Christina. "Course Correction: MED Series Helps Health System Make U-turn." *MGMA Connexion* 4, no. 4 (2004): 31–32.

Powell, Jennifer Heldt. "U.S. Health Administration Costly." *Modern Healthcare* (August 21, 2003).

Reinhardt, U. "The Social Perspective," in *Effectiveness and Outcomes in Health Care,* K. Heithoff & K. Lohr, eds. (Washington, D.C.: National Academy Press, 1990).

Robbins, Stephen P. *Organizational Theory Structure Design & Applications,* 3rd ed. (Englewood Cliffs, N.J.: Prentice Hall, 1990), 191, 249.

Royer, Thomas C. "Good Doctor/Good Leader." *MGMA Connexion* 3, no. 8 (2003): 26–27.

Schneck, Lisa H. "Governance Forms the Framework for a Group's Decision." *MGMA Connexion* 4, no. 5 (2004): 35–36.

———. "On Board or Bored Stiff? How to Run Effective Board Meetings." *MGMA Connexion* 3, no. 10 (2003): 54–55.

Shewhart, Walter A. *Statistical Methods from the Viewpoint of Quality Control* (New York: W. Edwards Deming, Dove Publications, 1986).

Showalter, J. Stuart. *The Law of Healthcare Administration,* 3rd Ed. (Chicago: Health Administration Press, 1999).

Singleton, Robin W. "Share and Share Alike: Three Problems Medical Groups Have in Common." *MGMA Connexion* 3, no. 3 (2003): 18–20.

"Six Sigma Systems." Six Sigma Systems, Overland Park, KS (June 2001), www.sixsigmasystems.com/what_is_six_sigma.html, (retrieved Feb. 1, 2006).

Thompson, James D. *Organizations and Action* (New York: McGraw Hill, 1967).

Turzillo, S. "Total Quality Management in the Medical Practice: The Road Seldom Traveled." ACMPE professional paper (Englewood, Colo.: American College of Medical Practice Executives, 1992).

Veney, J. E. *Statistics for Health Policy and Administration Using Microsoft Excel* (San Francisco: Jossey-Bass, 2003).

Wagner, S. F. *Introduction to Statistics* (New York: Harper Perennial, 1991).

Wagner, Stephen L. "The Organization and Operations of the Medical Group Practice," in *Physician Practice Management: Essential Operational Knowledge*, Lawrence Wolper, ed. (Boston, Mass.: Jones and Bartlett Publishers, 2005).

Wennberg, John. "Supplier Induced Demand and Small Area Variation." *Science* 182 (1973): 1102–1108.

Woolhandler, Steffie, Terry Campbell, & David U. Himmelstein. "Costs of Health Care Administration in the United States and Canada." *New England Journal of Medicine* 349 (August 21, 2003): 768–775.

About the Author

Stephen L. Wagner, PhD, FACMPE, lives in Charlotte, North Carolina, and serves as the vice president of the Carolinas Healthcare Systems, Physicians Network and is administrator of The Sanger Clinic, one of the largest cardiovascular medical practices in the United States. It is one of the only practices that integrates the full range of cardiovascular services – surgical and medical, pediatric and adult – under one organization. He has been active in the field of health care as an executive, teacher, and researcher for more than 30 years. He currently teaches health care management in the Seton Hall University Online MHA program and also serves as the executive mentor for the Online Master of Healthcare Administration Program.

Dr. Wagner holds a master's degree in Healthcare Fiscal Management from the University of Wisconsin–Madison School of Business and a Ph.D. from the University of Louisville's College of Business in Healthcare Public Policy Analysis. Dr. Wagner's principal areas of emphasis are in medical practice administration, medical economics, senior and community health, international medicine, new health care and educational technologies, as well as health care policy.

His past research has focused on outcome measurement for cardiovascular services, cardiovascular health, and on the development of health care systems in underserved communities, both domestic and international. Dr. Wagner has been involved in establishing medical practices and community services in St. Petersburg, Russia.

Dr. Wagner is a Fellow in the American College of Medical Practice Executives and has served as its examination committee chair.

Index